Motherhood & Manolos

KATE KERRIGAN

Copyright © 2010 Author Name

All rights reserved.

ISBN: 1477517340
ISBN-13: 9781477517345

TO MY THREE BOYS

Niall, Leo and The Tominator

CONTENTS

MOTHERHOOD, MARRIAGE, FAMILY
MANOLOS
AT LARGE
MY PERFECT LIFE

ABOUT THE AUTHOR

Kate Kerrigan is a best-selling novelist and one-time magazine editor (as Morag Prunty she edited, among others, Just Seventeen, more! magazine and Irish Tatler) who left the busy media whirlwind of London and Dublin to pursue her dream of raising a family in the Irish countryside. A popular newspaper columnist (The Sunday Tribune and Irish Mail) this is an edited collection of her writings reflecting on what happens when you get yourself the perfect life – only to find out that there's no such thing.

www.katekerrigan.ie

MOTHERHOOD, MARRIAGE, FAMILY
(and other acts of reckless insanity)

On Getting Pregnant When You're Not Expecting It

I had waited for my second pregnancy for seven long years and, in my mid forties, it was totally unexpected.

I was thirty-seven when Leo was born. It was the classic Bridget Jones scenario: the last minute rush in my mid-thirties to find a man, get married and have a child. On my wedding day I walked down the aisle followed by my six bridesmaids and five foot feathered train quite literally sobbing with relief. After a fraught two years of trying to conceive we finally got a result. I was so overjoyed that a part of me is still standing, shocked, in the bathroom of our first home, a small cottage in Dublin, looking at the thick blue line.

"We'll have to get a four door," my understated husband joked when I ran the mile to his office to tell him.

Nine months later Leo was born by Caesarean section. My first thought when he came out was, "This is why I am here. This is what I was born for."

Niall and I were confident, natural parents, suiting ourselves and making up our own rules as we went along. Leo was a happy, intelligent child. We wanted to do it again. There followed five years of tentative hope.

I made a decision not to get hung up on conceiving again. I had tests and there was no reason it couldn't happen naturally, except that I was pushing forty. I didn't want to put myself or my husband through the uncertain trauma of IVF or force the issue. I didn't want to make myself miserable because of something I wasn't meant to have, especially when I had already been gifted with one beautiful child.

However, the pull for another crack at motherhood was always there, the failure of it pinching at me.

There were thin blue lines, barely visible on the test-sticks. Holding onto my private elation, playing with dates – three weeks, four weeks, five weeks old - if it holds this time it'll be born in September, March, June. Then the disappointment of my ordinary blood would come.

I finally let go after about five years. We were on a package holiday with my sister and her family in Ibiza. I was late. I can't remember by how long.

"I'm a bit late."

That's all I ever said to Niall and he would nod acknowledgement that he had heard me, and that was that. We never discussed it or made a meal out of it. What was the point?

I was sitting by the pool in an atrocious blue bikini that I had bought back in the days when I was slim. Leo had refused to go to kiddie camp with his cousins and was splashing in the shallow pool. Niall and my sister were smoking and drinking coffee and I was considering getting my third *café con leche* of the day.

I felt a rumbling and ran up to our room without saying anything.

My sister followed me up and found me sitting on the edge of the hotel bed, its institutional coverlet stained red.

"Are you all right?" she asked.

"No," I said.

She put her arm around me and I cried, but it didn't feel right crying for something that wasn't real yet. I wasn't going to grieve for a lost dream. I had turned my desire for a second child into an indulgent idea fuelled by hormones.

"That's the end of it now," I said, "I give up."

So we contented ourselves as being parents of a "onesy" and poured everything into our cool, adorable prince of a son, Leo. After a while we became not just resigned to our family not growing, but pleased about it. We made plans to move to a smaller eco-house – a custom built home for just we three. As Leo grew older I could see myself having the freedom to travel, the money to retire young. Trips to the hair salon, shopping days away – as Leo grew up – I was starting to get some "me" time back. Another child would only disrupt the easy routine our small family had fallen into.

At the beginning of January 2009, sporting my usual post-Christmas paunch, I headed up to Dublin for a couple of days of pottering about.

On the last night I stayed with my friend Paul. Caustic, and never one to let a chance to tease me pass by, he made comment when I complained to him that my booted feet were unusually cold.

"Maybe you're pregnant," he said, "those boots look a bit strained about the calf dear!"

Early the following morning, I got the train back to Mayo.

I picked up the jeep in Ballina and drove into our village. Instead of turning right along the Quay where we live, I headed straight up the hill, and parked outside the chemist shop. The chemist has strange opening hours and I said to myself - if it's open I'll run in and get a pregnancy test. If not – I won't bother. It was and I did – the oblong box was a whopping eleven euro. What a waste of money, I thought, annoyed with myself for indulging this whim on the strength of Paul's stupid teasing. I couldn't remember when my last period had been, but I was forty- four and they were getting a bit erratic anyway. It was probably "the other thing". It was too early and too melodramatic to put a word on it yet, but I wasn't getting any younger.

I said a quick 'hi' to Niall, then went upstairs, peed on the stick (thinking to myself – "I am literally flushing eleven euro down the toilet here") and started to unpack my case.

I forgot about it for a while, and when I went back into the bathroom a few minutes later and saw it sitting on the window sill I gave it a cursory glance.

Two lines, one thick one.

That can't be right.

I looked at the box, then at the stick.

It wasn't a spindly thin thread either- this was big hullo-how-are-you stripe.

I stood at the top of the stairs and called down to Niall.

"Come up here love – I need you to look at something."

"What is it?" he said crossly as he walked into the bedroom.

"Look at this," I said handing him the stick and the box.

He looked from one to the other before thrusting it back at me saying; "I don't know- you're the woman."

The two of us stood there in silence for a few seconds, not knowing how to react, exactly. It was, of course, true. We knew it must be because the stick never lies. We were shocked into a kind of delighted disbelief.

"Go and get another one," Niall said.

"I'll go and see Doctor Joe in the morning," and we left it at that.

"I think I'm pregnant."

"Have you done the test?"

"Two."

"Were they both positive?"

"Yes."

"Congratulations!" Doctor Joe came out from behind his desk to give me a hug.

"Well done," he said, "Wait 'til I see Niall, the old dog!"

That, it seemed, was that.

I was weak with anxiety.

"I'm so old," I said, "What if something goes wrong? What should I be doing? Will it be ok? I'm forty four. I'll be forty five when the baby is born. It's too old. *I'm* too old."

I had not dared dream this would ever happen again. The thought of it going wrong, losing it, even at this early stage was unbearable.

"I'm really worried, Joe."

"Don't be ridiculous," he said. "You don't drink, or smoke – you're in great shape – I'd worry much less about you than I would most women in their thirties."

My expression must have done little to re-assure him.

"You'll be fine," he said as I was leaving, "and stop telling people how bloody old you are," he said as I was leaving.

Tom came three weeks early and without a hitch on 24th August, and was born by Caesarean section. Immediately he came out I called "Is he OK?"

I had chosen not to have any tests, despite as an old mother having been repeatedly offered them. I told myself, it would not have made a difference. This baby was a miracle and if it had special needs, well then I would still love it and care for it. At the same time I hadn't wanted to put myself in a position where my commitment to this pregnancy would be tested.

"He's perfect," the doctor said, "a perfect baby boy."

I couldn't believe it - that God had been so good or that we had been so lucky.

I told Niall to go over to the station where they were cleaning the infant up. I didn't want the baby to be apart from either one of us for one second. I strained my head to look at Niall, his face swollen with emotion, eyes soft and surging with love. He seemed less shocked, more confident that he was at Leo's birth- a seasoned father. The midwife bought baby Tom over, swaddled and clean and pushed him into my neck. He was so close that I could not see his face, this tiny and sweet creature like an infant bird, eyes closed, silent murmuring mouth, at the very beginning of life, unsullied perfection. From my belly to my shoulder in less than half an hour, at the end of the shortest, longest journey he would ever make. I kissed the side of his wrinkled pink face and apologised for crying all over him. My brand new boy was here. I was breathless with joy.

 Being the mother of a baby in my mid forties was easier than I had imagined. I had the money and the contacts for the best childcare, and although I frightened myself by calculating that I will be sixty-five before he finishes his education, I was infinitely more laid back and less neurotic than I was with our first son. I was not afraid to stick him in his play-pen in front of the telly so I could have a shower, and it wasn't the end of the world if he ate his lunch out of jar. Being older meant that I had a more laissez-faire attitude towards parenthood and that is why, I believe, he was an easy, good-humoured baby. Also, I was more independent. I realized that this little creature was only on loan to me for as long as he needed me. At ten months, Tom was already flying about – already more interested in poking at the dog and eating twigs than clinging to my breast. Having fulfilled my urgent ambition to be a mother with Leo, I enjoyed the freedom of knowing that this child needed me more than I needed him. He is a temporary gift and I enjoy each moment I have with him to the full.

 It makes me sad when single, childless women say that my late pregnancy has given them hope, because the one thing I do believe is that having a healthy pregnancy and a perfect child at forty-five is not the norm. I still envy younger mothers the freedom they will have when they are my age and have their children reared.

 I was tired a lot of the time – working and baby-minding were the only things I did. The "me time", social life, travel and dream eco-house went by the wayside. I worry about my health and his future, that I won't have always have the energy to be the good mother I want to be for both my sons. Then I bring myself back into the day - I look at my baby boy and I feel the exception of his existence rush through me in a flood of gratitude. I am renewed every time he smiles at me, I forget I am tired and know that I will have the energy to love and cherish both my boys until the day I die – and that will just have to be long enough.

KATE KERRIGAN

On Mooning Over Other People's Babies in Public

It is such a rare treat for me to have to get dressed up in proper clothes and have business lunches in Dublin – driving in the dark to Ballina at six am, humming along to Maxi, tearing out my heated rollers in the train station car park – facing into a whole day away from my boys. A day when I am free from the wife/mother tag and get to be a bona-fide working woman, someone who wears jackets with lapels and proper shoes and lipstick – *during the day*! And not just Mammy in a track-suit littered with biscuit crumbs who happens to write books on the kitchen table in-between the ferrying and feeding and general flustering about that is our family life.

My solitary trips to Dublin always start with such a sense of excitement. A posh restaurant for lunch! *Vanity Fair* on the train home! A sushi box from Aya which I'll have guzzled before Athlone. Hell, the details don't matter. It's an uninterrupted day to myself. Bliss.

My husband wanted me to get the new three thirty train home. "You'll be back by seven," he said hopefully, "in time for dinner."

Exactly, I thought. Walking straight into baby-mash and bathtime and three grumpy, expectant faces. "I'll try," I said, "but I can't promise anything."

"Just say," he argued, "just say it's really important you get the three thirty. Put your foot down." Put *your* foot down you mean, I thought.

"It's an important meeting," I said, "It's *work.*" So I loitered over lunch and rang to say I'd be back on the later train.

"How's the baby?" I said.

"He won't settle."

Once, just once, I thought, why can't you say, "We're all fine. You go relax and enjoy yourself," even if it's not true, like I do when *you* go away.

I went and spent too much money on a tracksuit top, as a reward for getting more work but more as an act of indulgent self-destruction as in the midst of an agreed economy drive. I dropped in on a friend in their office and moaned at them for an hour then got to the station an hour too early. One whole hour, and no platform announced yet. I went and loitered about in Eason's, spending far too long deciding on which magazines I could 'afford' after splurging on the top.

As I was noting miserably that I had already read most of them in the hairdressers the week before, I stepped back and bumped into a woman and her enormous double buggy. "Sorry," I said, then instinctively, unable to stop myself, I leaned in for a look- beautiful twin girls. Perfect, smooth brown skin and pink pouting mouths.

"They're beautiful," I said. She smiled back, vaguely, still fingering her magazine. Doubtless unimpressed by the patronizing approval of some nice middle-class white stranger. My hands hovered over the nearest one's chubby cheek, and I remember my sister, back in my broody years, reprimanding me murderously for touching the newborns of strangers in café's. "Parents don't like that," she said. "It's invasive – you'll give them germs!"

I went back out into the concourse and downed a Butlers Hot Chocolate and had a little petulant cry. I texted my husband. "I miss you. I love you. I'm sorry I'm late. I hate being away." I didn't send it because I knew he'd get cross. Every time I go away on business trip there is always a tearful phone call soon after I arrive. Whenever I feel lonely I get angry with him for not being there, even when it is me who has gone away. I take a break from my children to stay sane, but the moment they are not within touching distance, I feel bereft. It is the irrational nature of familial love. Fishfingers for dinner, arguments over *Lewis* or *Top Gear*, moaning over homework, running out of baby-wipes during the most spectacular poo of the week - the everyday familiarity of the same small challenges, living with the same people's habits.

Family life can be wearing, and is something I sometimes feel I need to escape. Then I see a stranger's baby in a buggy and I remember the longing I had through my twenties and much of my thirties for an ordinary family life. I want to rush home to my husband and my two sons to fight and feed and sling about trying to write books while my husband tuts over my spilled biscuit crumbs and not worry about high heels or lipstick or spending money on nice tops that won't make any difference.

So next time some lady looks into my buggy and coos over my magnificent baby I will remind myself that I am living my dream. And I will ask her if she would like to touch his cheek.

On Falling in Love with My Mother

I often (but not too often) joke that if I ever left my husband it would not be for another man, but for my mother. I fell in love with my mother again in my early 30s and we are markedly close.

Through my 30s and 40s my mother has become a companion and friend as well as a supportive and nurturing parent. One of the things that surprises me about our relationship is how coveted it is among my friends. Not just our relationship, but my mother herself.

"I wish my mum was more like your mum." "I wish I could talk to my mother the way you talk to yours." "Your mum is so much fun . . . I wish my mum was as open-minded as yours." And bizarrely, "I want to get your mum around so that some of her will 'rub off' on my mum."

And yet I think this says more about the attitude we have towards our mothers than it does about the mothers themselves.

My mother, while she does have exceptional qualities, is not so different from her peers as my friends perceive. It is the fact that I have made an effort to treat her as a woman and not just a mother that has allowed our, in the past, often fraught mother-daughter relationship to flourish into a deep friendship.

Throughout my teens and right up to the end of my 20s I held my mother responsible for everything that went wrong in my life: my inability to form a satisfactory relationship with a man, my bad teeth/feet/legs and fluctuating weight. I once lost my passport the night before an important business trip and rang her in the middle of my panic to blame her for being a hoarder herself and not training me to be more organised.

The biggest thing I blamed my mother for was the gap inside me that craves love. That hole is just part of the human condition but one which we try to fill with drink, or food, or sex or therapy . . . seeking the satisfaction of complete fulfilment which we will never find. The only love that is big enough to fill that gap is surely a mother's love. However it's not until you become a mother yourself that you realise the hard truth which is that no matter how big your love is for your child, ultimately they will have to make it on their own.

My turning point with my mother came when I was 31. I was staying in my mother's house in London. I was unemployed, single and childless and my youngest sister had just become pregnant by her boyfriend. I would like to say I had conflicted feelings, but that would be too kind. I was furious and bitterly, bitterly jealous. My mother came into my room early one morning and found me howling, pounding the wall shouting, "It should have been me!"

She gathered me into her arms and comforted me. I realised then that there was no other human being on earth who would ever love me enough to sympathise with such ugly feelings. And crucially, I realised I still needed her as a mother. I made a conscious decision to let all of the past go and form a new relationship with this person. This woman who had all this love towards me: how would it be if I didn't dismiss her love as a given but took it on afresh? What would happen if, instead of the immature expectation I had always had of this cure-all love, that my mother should be able to intuit my every need otherwise she had failed, I started to ask for her love, ask for her advice? And crazier still, actually listen to it and perhaps even, from time to time, take it on board. I have traced the most successful, the happiest and the most secure days of my adult life back to the moment I started to do that.

One such occasion was in Yamamori on George's Street in 1997. I asked her what she thought of my relatively new live-in boyfriend.

"I think you should marry him."

I was taken aback . . . this was the woman who told me never to get married. Why this one? I asked.

She took me back to an incident that had occurred a few weeks before. A friend of mine from London was staying in our apartment in Dublin along with Niall and my mother. My mother and my friend were both en route to somewhere else, and I got called away for work. I was nervous about how Niall would deal with these relative strangers as none of them knew the other very well. Tragedy struck during the night when my friend got a phone call from London to say his mother, whom he lived with, had died. It was a terrible shock.

My mother described to me how Niall had handled the situation calmly, with strength, sensitivity and great compassion.

"He stayed up all night talking to the poor man," she said. "Now that's the sort of person you want to be married to. And oh, "she added, "he's a hard worker."

My mother had always actively discouraged her daughters from getting married, saying the institution was outdated and designed to tie women down.

What was this turnaround all about?

"I've changed my mind, "she said. "I know I have always said the opposite but now I would like to see you married with a child. I can see that's what you desperately want and I think it would make you happy so I want it for you too."

An English journalist, slightly older than me, recently interviewed my mother and I and was astonished at the cultural differences in our respective lives.

The journalist had grown up at the same time as me, in London, but her British baby-boomer parents were living the '60s dream. They were doing the whole dope-smoking, nudie flower power pop songs thing while my mother and her emigrant peers were still held in the cloying, guilty grip of the Catholic church. They wore the long flowery skirts and the platform shoes but they left the free-love principles behind. They eschewed contraception but remained loyal to wedding vows, even through being battered by alcoholic husbands, and stayed at home cooking and cleaning and minding their children because they didn't have the confidence to avail of the education and the work opportunities now available to them. While the world around them partied, the majority of my mother's generation of Irish emigrants spent the '60s and '70s picking rusk crumbs out of their Draylon-covered sofas in the London suburbs, cooking big dinners for tired husbands, feeding babies and taking their daughters to Irish dancing classes in chilly church halls.

Joan Baez was singing on their kitchen transistor about revolution. Erica Jong, the Female Eunuch, Gloria Steinem, free thinking, free love… it seemed like everyone was free except them. The revolution was happening on their doorsteps but not in their homes, they could smell the freedom but they couldn't taste it. So they drummed into their daughters these messages of independence. "See the world, have your own money, don't worry about getting married and having children. Any fool can get married; don't sell yourself short."

They bred a generation of independent career women with aching ovaries. Like Bridget Jones, it seemed finding a good husband and having children later in life was not as easy as our mothers told us it would be. For those of us who managed to squeeze it in, "having it all" became "doing it all". As Germaine Greer recently said, "When we said we 'wanted it all' . . . it seems what we got 'all' of was the work."

I think our mothers' generation has straddled a wider gap in the culture of women's personal and working lives than any other.

The gap between my life and my grandmother's life is culturally colossal, yet I hope my generation does as good a job of bridging the gap between our children's lives and our parents.

I also think my generation of women are particularly hard on our mothers. We urge them to be more liberal, more like us. And yet they have witnessed and weathered the almost complete disintegration of their value system whilst still managing to fling their daughters forward into a new era, fuelling us with their dreams as well as their disappointments.

What I have discovered through my mother and her friends in the past 15 years is that these women, with a tremendous amount to offer, often lack the confidence to achieve their potential. What makes them more hard-done by than the generations before them is that liberation was within their grasp . . . but their arms were not long enough to reach it.

My mother could have been a novelist and the confidence she lacked to do it herself, she made sure she gave to me. That has been her gift to me as a writer: not just her encouragement and support, but her unfulfilled writer's permission to mine her life for the stories she could have told if she had grown up in a more modern time.

The man my mother 'chose' for me was also sexy and funny and I was in love with him. But ultimately the foundation of the happiness I have experienced being married to him has been down to the qualities she saw in him straight away, strength of character, kindness and a powerful work ethic.

My mother isn't always right, but then, neither am I. However, she is always older and often, very often, much wiser than I am. And she loves me. Surely they are the best qualifications a good friend and mentor could have.

On Competitive Parenting

One of the few things that does not appear to have pervaded Irish social culture from the UK or US (yet!) is competitive parenting. I only know about it, really, because my sister lived with it in London before she, wisely, upped sticks and moved here where the culture around children remains more casual.

"What do you mean he's not potty trained!" she would yelp at me panic-stricken whilst shovelling home-made organic baby food into her youngest, terrified that proximity to an unpotty-trained two-and-a-half-year-old nephew could result in social ostracisation. And in middleclass English society it does.

Ditto America - shortly after a New York friend moved here she informed me that her two-year old would be bilingual in Irish/English by the time she was four because she was going to Trinity College under pain of death. I told her if she carried on like that she would have a lap-dancing heroin addict on her hands by the age of 14 - her relief was palpable and our friendship was sealed.

From the vantage point of not having to be a competitive mother, I rather approve of it. There are worse things to compete over than one's ability to be a good parent, like the size of your house, the make of your car or the pertness of your breasts - all of which seem to be ambitions we have heartily (and depressingly) embraced. We have "yummy mummies" - Brown Thomas babes with cavernous multi-pocketed baby bags and SUVs - but they are buying their homemade cookies and flavoured breads in Avoca - the easy way out.

In other, more developed Western cultures there is a timetable by which your child should be sleeping through the night, weaned, on solids, using a potty, walking, talking, reading, writing, wiping their own bottom, etc. If you waver a few months before or after these important milestones you will either gain the respect of the other mothers as a "Supermom" or be reviled as a "Bad Mother". It is control freakery at its most impressive. At last - something tangible and terrible to worry about for the sake of it. Never mind the wrinkles and the cellulite, ladies - you might be poisoning your child if you do not feed him exclusively on homemade organic produce. If your child is not potty-trained at the right time or is weaned too early or too late, they could develop terrible psychological problems and end up in prison. Or therapy! You could be thwarting their future ambitions to be a doctor if you don't have them speaking Gaeilge fifteen minutes after exiting the womb. And that's before we've even started with the sewing and the baking.

Parents here are happy to just fling money at children's birthday parties, bowling, adventure parks, McDonalds - Thunder Road Café if you're posh - whatever. Oh no - this is not up to standard at all. What we Irish mothers need to whip us into shape is the high-maintenance home party.

   This is where you fix it for 30 little girls to sew themselves handbags made from bits of discarded denim and decorate them with buttons, sequins and patches which you have been collecting and cutting for the last three months. Or the camping party for all your son's classmates where each child goes home with a baked-bean billy-can soldered with his initials. This thing of shoving them in front of a DVD with a family pack of Tayto is just not good enough, ladies! It's time we got up to speed and finally embraced the truly neurotic nature of modern parenthood.

On Letting Your Kids Learn Independence

It was Sunday morning, and the day seemed mild enough and Leo and his friend Fin were harassing me. The two lads were sensible nine-year-olds, and knew everyone in the village. Leo was at that age where he started to crave a bit of independence, and we would sometimes send him down to the chip van at the end of the pier on his own once a week, although the convenience factor was diminished slightly by my standing at the front wall craning the two hundred yards to check on his progress there and back. Pete, my beloved supplier of the best fish and chips in Ireland, knew Leo and kept an eye out for him, and if was lashing with rain and there was a wait, he would send him home and drop our dinner down himself. It wasn't much of an adventure, really.

Leo and Fin would go up on outings to the local garage the odd time for sweets, but the play park, where they wanted to go on this particular day, was a good walk, there was a couple of roads to cross – and, well, I wasn't sure. I rang Fin's dad for advice and permission and he said, "No problem," so we compromised. I would drop them down in the car, go and pick my mother-in-law up from Crossmolina, twenty minutes away, and collect them on the way back. I left them with instructions not to talk to strangers, get bullied, bully anyone else, go outside the confines of the play area, etc.

The park was empty, "Hooray! The place to ourselves!" they shouted and I drove off. On the way up the hill through the village I almost turned back. It didn't feel right leaving them there on their own. But I trusted them and I had promised. I kept going but by the time I reached the half-way mark to Crossmolina my head was buzzing. What if I went back and they weren't there? Supposing they were abducted? I would never see my son again – how would I explain myself to Fin's parents? Perhaps some evil paedophile had seen me leave them there, small, vulnerable, unaccompanied children – and was at this very moment drugging them and putting them into a van to be trafficked. I pulled over to the side of the road, the sweat pouring off me, and rang Niall.

"Go and get them," I said, "I'm having a moment. At least go and check on them on your way into Tesco."

I felt slightly better for another five minutes, but before I reached my mother-in-law's it started to rain. They'd get wet! Fin had a bad chest- this could bring on an asthma attack! Did Leo's hoodie have a hood?

Then I remembered. I spent my whole childhood getting soaked through to the skin in unsuitable clothing. In winter I can clearly remember, at eleven years of age, standing frozen solid in the snow, wearing flimsy shoes and a school blazer, waiting hours for one of three buses to take me home, alone, from first year in secondary school. From as far back as I could walk, we played out on the street with the other kids, regularly calling into each other's houses, and often the houses of lonely adults for a chat and a biscuit. We were told not to talk to strangers, but we didn't really understand why. And when I acquired a middle-aged male stalker – a mysterious man in a grey coat and astrakhan hat who followed me to and from secondary school every day from the age of thirteen to fourteen – I didn't quite know what to do about it. I certainly couldn't tell my parents, and, while his presence sort of unnerved me, when he sat next to me on the bus one day I still chatted politely to him. Although, I said, I really didn't think it was a good idea for us to "meet-up" on our own.

Although I was young and vulnerable, I was also capable of keeping myself safe.

We had a play park near our house in London where we played unsupervised every day from as far back as I can remember. The parents didn't come and sit on benches and read the Sunday papers and drink Starbucks and make sure we weren't being abducted. They had got on with their daily lives and came looking for us if we weren't back in time for tea. Play-parks were for kids.

Now we live in a culture where childhood independence is taboo. I read a report of a father in the US who took his eye off his five-year-old in a play park for two minutes and the child ran into the road and was killed. In addition to the appalling grief and guilt, the man was convicted and served a sentence for involuntary manslaughter. He was only as negligent as any parent is from time to time in taking their eyes off a toddler for a few seconds. The tragedy was the kind of appalling freak of fate all parents dread, yet our fear-mongering society holds him responsible.

In actual fact crime in the Western world is actually lower than it was when most of us were growing up. There is no reality-based reason that children today should be treated as more helpless and vulnerable than we were when we were young. We are so overprotective of our children that an American journalist, Lenore Skenazy, was accused of being the Worst Mom In The World after allowing her nine-year-old boy to ride the New York subway alone. The freedom she allowed him in doing so was not an act of neglect, but a deliberate, carefully considered act of parenting to acknowledge her child's growing desire for independence, and encourage him to see the world as a safe place to live, as opposed to "the world is a dangerous place" culture depicted by the media, seemingly to no other end but to put the fear of God in parents. In reality, Skenazy argues that, "Mostly, the world is safe. Mostly, people are good. To emphasize the opposite is to live in the world of tabloid TV. A world filled with worst-case scenarios, not the world we actually live in, which is factually, statistically, and, luckily for us, one of the safest periods for children in the history of the world."*

Skenazy's parenting ethos makes a lot of sense, based as it is on the idea that is a parents job to teach our children how to get along in the world rather than coddle them, because "...the coddled child will not have Mom or Dad around all the time. Adults once knew what we have forgotten today. Kids are competent. Kids are capable. Kids deserve freedom, responsibility, and a chance to be part of the world."

Amen to that, although it didn't quite stop me from half-heartedly considering fitting Leo with an electronic abduction tag.

KATE KERRIGAN

On Other People's Children

I fell victim to summer love - with a little girl called Kelly Ann. With the long summer days stretched out in front of him, eight-year old Leo asked if his friend could come over and play. We have an open house policy on kids here. Because Leo doesn't have any siblings near his age, he has always relied on his friends for company. We're lucky because we live in a village so the precious two-hour invite-only playdate, a necessity of the enforced schedules of city life, doesn't apply. My friends and I pick each other's children up from school and bring them around to each other's houses where they eat and play and get thrown into the mash of somebody else's family life. All the children largely go the same school, and those friends that Leo doesn't see every day are a delightful novelty.

When I first became a mother I went through a brief period of thinking that I adored children – that I was a sort of earth mother type. I quickly realized that this was merely a symptom of the temporary flood of love that came with having my own child. I am not a children person. Although I hasten to add, neither am I a curmudgeonly old bag who hates all kids except her own, and I do consider that children should be treated with more care than adults (who, in theory at least, can look after themselves and should often know better), but at the end of the day children are individuals, and like adults, some are more lovable than others.

Perhaps it is the fact that my mother was a teacher, but egocentric parents who assume that their child is eminently adorable to everyone irritate me. I remember a mother once complaining to me, after a school parent meeting where the teacher had commented that her 5-year-old child was easily distracted and didn't pay attention. She was scandalized and took it as a personal insult by the teacher.

"It's appalling," she bristled, "Where's the nurturing?" she complained to me.

"That would be your job," I pointed out, irritated by the notion that essential early years education is considered a kind of state child-minding service. It is not the teacher's job to love the children, only to educate them. It is our job as a collective society, and as individuals, to respect and care about the welfare of all children. It is not our responsibility to love them all. That is the parent's job. If your child isn't getting enough attention, or is watching too much television, or is not getting enough exercise, or is eating the wrong foods – it is your fault, not the child-minder or the teachers.

Anyway – I am lucky in that most of my friends have children that I adore and Leo's friends are almost exclusively attractive, well-mannered kids. But little Kelly-Ann was a real poppet. She was a tiny, delicate looking child with long, unruly nut-brown hair that refused to stay in a plait. She was bursting with confidence and joie-de-vivre – and on her first visit to our house made me feel like this was the most exciting, enthralling experience she had ever had in her life (which it undoubtedly wasn't!). The two of them came and begged for Kelly to sleepover after her first day here. "We can have a DVD night!" she said, enthusing me into gathering duvets and settling the two of them into a cosy nest in the playroom until gone ten. When I eventually coaxed them up to Leo's room, they sat in their respective beds reading quietly like an old married couple until they feel asleep. Around midnight she wandered into our bedroom where we were watching TV, causing my shocked husband to modestly pull the duvet up over his bare chest.

"I can't sleep," she said. Not upset or tearful, just quite matter-of-factly. "Please may I have the light on?"

"No problem," I said, and scooped her back up into Leo's precious bunk bed (he has never volunteered it for anyone before) and tucked her in.

"It's a bit scary sleeping over somewhere for the first time, Kelly, isn't it?"

"Yes," she said, "a little," but there was no drama. She had made the decision to stay, and tomorrow was another day and she had been promised pancakes for breakfast.

"You're a great girl, Kelly," I said, "I'm so glad you came to stay," and as I left her little hand poked out from between the wooden slats and I gave it a squeeze. She was asleep in five minutes.

On the Santa Clause

There were only forty-three shopping days left, and the shops' shelves are already groaning under the weight of all those cinnamon-scented candles and holly-festooned 'quality' biscuit tins which you would immediately put in a cupboard and forget about.

What's that you say? Too early? Not feeling festive yet? It's obscenely commercial nowadays and all you got in your day was an orange and were glad of it?

Personally, I can't wait. I've already started my countdown to Christmas and am already searching out themes for my tree in interiors magazines and wondering whether to repeat last year's successful chestnut and apricot stuffing or try something new. Of course, the thing that makes Christmas really special is the little ones, isn't it? The look on their adorable little faces at 7am when they have already consumed three-quarter of a Cadbury's selection stocking and are tearing open the gifts it took you six weeks to source and pay for, harassing you for batteries before casting them aside in favour of a pound-shop trinket in their stocking.

How do we ever get through it!

However, there may be some solace to be found from that most unexpected of corners . . . the North Pole. For those of you parents out there who are counting down to The Late Late Toy Show and the horrendous crush to equip your beloved offspring with their heart's desire that ensues, let me tell you of a new initiative that Santa Claus's office is has launched.

I learned about Santa's New Ruling when our gentle and easily pleased five-year-old started school in September, with the result that he gradually transmogrified into one of those tantruming horrors that you see in the supermarket and think, "That's the parents' fault." It's quite common, apparently.

Seemingly, after five hours of being good in a school uniform he liked to let rip. "It's because he can," my retired-teacher mother informs me.

Nothing heavy, you understand, just lots of "I hate you" and "I want" and other stuff that made we naive parents of one single child panic and wonder where we had failed. (Parents of two are generally smug and knowing of these things. Parents of three always just seem harassed and rather cross with themselves for having got cocky and thinking they could manage more than two . . . or having been stupid and celebrated the birth of their much wanted second child with sex. Parents of four, five or over are invariably gloriously laidback.) So that year Santa stepped up his Campaign for Good Children.

The year before, it was just a general "You'd better be good" verbal warning. Sometimes we would point out one of his spies watching us if we were bordering on a restaurant tantrum or had forgotten to say 'thank-you' to a shopkeeper. But that year Santa's office was going to do spot-checks, like the VAT inspector, on a random number of five-year-olds across the world.

Imagine our surprise when we got one the week after Halloween, which is when the first batch of 'Official Warnings' go out. It came in the form of an email on Daddy's computer. Daddy's a graphic designer and was very impressed with Santa's new logo and corporate image. The email was a warning.

Our son would get his requested presents, but he had to keep up his end of the bargain. He had to start eating vegetables between then and Christmas and please and thank-you were to be re-introduced. No more hating anybody . . . most especially his wonderful parents who were, according to Mr Claus, exemplary.

What else did he say? Oh yes, no more 'I wants, play nicely with his cousins, no saying bad words, no whining, go to bed on time, sharing. That about covered it. It's hard to explain how Santa suddenly had all this personal information at his fingertips except that that year he joined forces with Holy God.

Holy God sees everything so there is no getting away with anything, anything at all, between then and the end of December. Next year, if it was a success, Santa was thinking of stepping it up to six, maybe even seven-year-olds. Now, at last, I have a reason for the Christmas season to come early.

And people say children are manipulative. Anyone got the number of a good therapist? I think there's a lad around here might need one in about 20 years' time.

On Keeping My Mother Alive

Mum wouldn't stop pottering. I had taken her home from Castlebar hospital where she had been treated for a broken arm. So many of my friends' elderly parents are in hospital, sick or dying and "they had a fall" is often what the last leg to the grave starts off with.

"What happened?" Everyone had been asking with concern (my Mum is a popular lady), expecting the usual – slipped in her way out of the shower, tripped on the stairs scenario. "She was playing tennis on holiday in Portugal," I'd confess, "in flip flops," then wait for the cheery, "Good for her!"

Her arm looked nasty in the X-ray, and the doctor on duty in Castlebar Outpatients said he could fix it – maybe even that afternoon, certainly the next day, with a simple operation. So we booked her there and then – on Monday – and the following Friday, after many broken promises and one last-minute cancellation after the pre-meds were taken, she was finally done. Mum doesn't mind hospitals, and we could have taken her home, but she was happy there with her meals being served up to her on a tray and all the papers spread out on the bed. It was a nice rest for her. She said, "I've got nothing to do – it's great!" and besides, her arm was very sore and they could dole her out painkillers on demand.

My sister Claire and I were nervous wrecks. It is a sad day for the health service when you are more afraid of getting sick in the hospital than you are relieved at getting well. MRSA is now so commonplace in Castlebar that one almost expects a loved one to contract it as a matter of course. I kept bringing her in pro-biotic yogurts and drinks to build up her immune system. The broken arm would probably heal itself after six to eight weeks in a sling, but if she caught a deadly hospital bug because I had persuaded her to take the fast-track surgical route, I wouldn't be able to live with myself.

Claire brought her tubes of that awful alcohol hand rub we were all using during the swine flu scare. *"Please rub your hands with the dispensers provided. Please rub your hands with the dispensers provided,"* the electronic voice loop at the revolving hospital door ominously reminded me as I went in and out for another cigarette. I used every one that I passed, not really understanding the logic of it.

The nurses were lovely, Mum said – and the food wasn't bad, but then my mother is a particularly glass-half-full person.

Less than thirty hours after the operation Claire and I took her home, both of us almost weeping with relief. She found our fears of her picking up a bug ridiculous – but then, I nag her continuously about the rugs she has scattered all over the house. "Death-traps Mum – you'll trip and I'll find you lying at the bottom of the stairs one day and *I'll never get over it!*" Appealing to her maternal duties is the only thing that works. "I suppose…" she said, looking at some beloved John Lewis rug she took great pains to carry back in a suitcase from England.

Once she arrived home, she was forced entirely under the care of her two beady-eyed, bossy daughters. She had her sling, and her physio exercises and her pain-relief and her instructions for the GP and next appointment. I stayed with her the first night and the next morning I came back from getting her prescription and I caught her about to carry a load of washing upstairs with her one good arm. I had such a go at her that she half-tripped on the bottom stair in her rush to get back up to bed.

Mam is such a vital, lively woman. She had never injured herself before, and thrived through a double hip operation ten years ago. She's pretty sensible with herself generally (the tennis incident gives the impression that she is sporty, but in actual fact it was a reckless one-off incident, unlikely to be repeated and there is no need to worry).

When you love somebody you want to keep them close to you for as long as you can. In my mid-forties our mother/daughter relationship feels as if it is only reaching its prime. Nursing her through this hiccup I felt, not only a fear of losing her, but the privilege of how much I love her. I want to be able to give her back some of the caring that's her due, and be a living testament to the extraordinary mother she is, and continues to be, to me.

But I'll have to learn to curb my anxiety and work on my bedside manner.

On Wanting to Watch Telly When I Should Be Watching My Child

Our baby Tommo was like a scurrying hamster and I couldn't take my eyes off him for one second. A small testosterone tank, he was mad to get out of his playpen (or 'prison', as we aptly call it) and get on with the great adventure of exploring our big old house. There are drawers to be opened, taps to be turned on, cupboards to climb into and of course, the Everest of every self-respecting toddler's ambitions: the stairs.

My own ambitions had altered to fit his. A year ago a facial followed by lunch with the girls and an afternoons shopping was an achievable luxury, now such a leisurely afternoon of "me" time looks like an ambition as unachievable as Everest itself. Bliss for me at the moment was be two hours sitting in bed watching a *Miss Marple* TV movie from the DVD boxed set I requested for my birthday, while Tommo crawled around the upstairs bedrooms having a good old root around looking for hairgrips he can choke himself on – please God to no avail.

The upstairs of the house is easier to childproof than downstairs because it's largely comprised of soft furnishing, clothes and laundry – as opposed to the downstairs which is where we keep all the "bad" stuff likes knives, and stoves and the heinous grot that lives under everyone's fridge, out of reach to every mop and Hoover, yet not to the tiny, flexible fingers of a curious crawler. In order for me to get my DVD-in-bed time, I had to eliminate the risk of my small child falling down the stairs and breaking his neck.

So it seemed too good to be true when my sister-in-law revealed that the Lidl catalogue had their good quality, cheap stair-gates coming in again that week. She had her son, lively one-year-old Amos, happily imprisoned in the first floor of her apartment in Dublin with the same.

I told Niall and he said, "Leave it for now – I need to measure the space."

I ignored him. He was trying to put things off, as usual.

So in a frenzied panic – as is the way with Lidl offers – I belted into Ballina and got the last four sets (hoorah!) filling the rest of the trolley with loo roll, olive oil, breaded frozen chicken, Greek yogurt, weirdly branded crisps – all the Lidl stuff I am incapable of leaving that shop without stocking up on.

Of course, when I got them home, the stair gates didn't fit. I read the box: "Will fit up to 109cm space with 7cm extensions."

Niall pleaded with me. "Leave this to me. I'll sort it out – he's not even walking yet. What's the mad rush?"

"He'll clamber up and kill himself," I said, "we have to do this now – today!"

What I meant of course was, "I want to watch Miss Marple in bed *now* with the same urgency with which I used to *have* to have that discount designer handbag. The same selfish impulse was driving me, but mothers aren't allowed to be selfish.

So I hared back to Lidl to get the extensions mentioned on the box. No extensions. I ran up to the local, much-more-expensive children's things shop where they sell stair-gates. They had one flimsy, very expensive stair gate left which would lock Tommo into the bedroom at least, but they were that bit too narrow and there were – no extensions!

I stood in the car park wondering what was the point of having an outlet the size of an airport hanger, packed twenty foot high with climbing frames and trampolines, if they never seemed to stock anything that I ever need. Should it be this hard, really? Being a consumer in a consumer driven world?

I rang Niall. "Get on the Internet and find me extensions for my Lidl stair-gates." He texted back with the news that they existed – but only in America.

"Argos and Littlewoods," I screamed – "NOW!"

Almost a week later the Lidl stair-gates were still sitting in my hallway, the wooden boxes in various states of undress after, in a fit of determination, I unpacked the twiddly bits to see if I could double them up and make them fit. If I don't get them back for a refund soon, there will be no refund and the whole thing will have been a complete waste of time and money. In the meantime Niall will order the stair-gates from Littlewoods, get them delivered and fit them, all in his own good time.

"If our son falls down the stairs and breaks his neck, it will be your fault…" I threaten, "…or burns himself on the stove, or cuts his finger off with a knife – I want him to play upstairs – it's safer."

"Nonsense," he says, "You just want to watch telly in bed."

On Parental Expectations

When he was two and a half my son announced that he wanted to be a doctor. I was self-effacement itself- oh don't take any notice, I'm sure he'll be a drug dealer, I'd say- but secretly I was thrilled stupid. He even worked it up a bit for me and said that his best friend Clare was going to be a vet and they were going to work out of the same building. He explained that people could bring their pets in and leave them with her while he made the humans better. Adorable yes? I bored a lot of people with that one.

Of course, I didn't believe him, except that when he told me this week that he wanted to be an artist and not a doctor any more I realised that I had become rather attached to the idea. Already. I think I might have actually said out loud, "Why don't you become a doctor and do 'art' in your spare time?" I did, because I remember how adamant he was about the art. I now know never to say it to him again, ever . . . or he will definitely drop out of art school and become a drug dealer.

The horrible irony is I am a writer and his father is a graphic designer. We get to be arty when we want him to be a 'professional'. Why?

Are doctors or accountants or lawyers any better than the rest of us? No. Are they richer than us in these days when you can't get hold of your plumber because he is holidaying in his golf resort villa in the Algarve? Not really. Are people who train in the professions any happier in themselves or in their marriages? Or any more intelligent or nicer as people than anybody else? In my honest and reasonably vast experience of people, no. Actually, emphatically not.

Secretly applauding my toddler for wanting to grow up and be a doctor is certainly one of the darkest confessions I have ever publicly made because it exposes me as having an element of the most tacky, tasteless of human failings which is, to my mind, snobbery.

Wanting your son to be a doctor puts one in the same region as thinking you are posher than somebody else because you have a better job, or a more 'refined' accent, or a bigger house. I don't think there is anything sadder than being a snob, except perhaps being a racist . . . which is, let's face it, little more than snobbery for people with very low self-worth.

But children will do that to you. Get inside your value system and wriggle it about until you find yourself caring about things that you never thought you would like organic food, the environment and getting a university education.

For any parent, the most important thing to them is their child's future. We all want our children to be successful, so we strive to give them the best education. But I wonder sometimes if our education system, which still puts too much value on exams, narrows our ideal of what "successful" is . . . the kudos of being a "professional" or the life skills required to be a rounded human being. Of course, it's not an either/or decision but if I had to choose for my child, I'd sacrifice the former for the latter any day.

On What I 'Need' In My Marriage

I remember flipping through a celebrity magazine one afternoon in a few years back which broadcasted the failings of not one, but two celebrity marriages. Brit and Kevin Federline had broken up, and a few pages later unnamed "friends" divulged that Reese Witherspooon's marriage to her lesser-known spouse had ended too. Speculation was that her young husband was finding it hard, living with an Oscar-winning success. Can't be easy that, especially when you are a lesser-known actor. Must be a real hardship. Maybe it's best to call it a day and leave the two small kids and the emotional carnage of a broken marriage behind than endure the humiliation of your wife being more successful than you.

And young Kevin's philandering suggested that he had fallen out of love with Britney . . . and there's no point in carrying on if that's the case. No point in staying in a marriage that's making you miserable.

Is it time we reassessed our definition of 'miserable' in a relationship? It comes down to the selfish manipulation of that phrase "having our needs met".

Here are a few of my needs: I need to start each day with my husband gazing at me with an expression of deep admiration and unbridled passion. I then need for him to get up and serve me a low-carb cooked breakfast. I need to know that loving and delightful thoughts about me are popping into my husband's head all day long whilst not distracting him from his work, because I need him to surprise me with romantic weekends away. I need him to tell me I am looking lovely every time I apply lipstick and sometimes when I don't. I need to be able to look at him every day and think, "Phwoar!" with the same voracity and lust I did when we were young lovers. I also need for my life partner never to irritate me, criticise me, or say a cross word to me, ever. Oh . . . and I need him to do all of these things whilst still behaving like a real man and not one of those weedy soft-fingered "new men". I need all of this every day, for the rest of my life as long as we both shall live.

Anyone else out there finding that marriage is not quite the contract we signed up for? The problem with being part of the privileged "Because I'm worth it" generation is that sometimes it is difficult to make that all important distinction between what we need (a standard issue spouse for sex and companionship) and what we want (see above, with all the trimmings of a Hollywood romance).

I believe in divorce. There are enough tragic terrible marriages out there to make it a necessary part of a civilised society. But I am not talking about physical and emotional abuse or serial adultery. I'm talking about the kind of everyday misery that every relationship involving two people living in close proximity to one another must experience. Here's the newsflash: a little misery in marriage is inevitable.

You don't have to encourage it, or welcome it, but you better learn to suck it up from time to time. We have mythologized love to such an extent that people are no longer prepared for the realities of long-term relationships. We are taught that it is good not to compromise, not to put up with anything we don't like, not to sacrifice our own beliefs for anyone or anything. Yet compromise and sacrifice are the cornerstones of marital love.

No matter what way you dress it up, the best thing you can bring to a marriage is not the feeling of 'being in love', but romance's poor relation: tolerance. Add to that enough maturity to be able to fulfil your own needs and you have some hope. Optimism and chemistry, which seem to be the bedrock of the modern marriage, just don't cut it, folks. And while I am pontificating, one more tip for the ladies: Try to find a man who has that most underrated of qualities: character. I did and so far my Oscar hasn't bothered him. Although I am still waiting for my cooked breakfast…

On The Husband's Bad Back

On our tenth wedding anniversary we were still reeling from the death of both our brothers within a few months of each other. I forgot, and Niall gave me a peck on the cheek before breakfast and reminded me.

The next year wasn't much a celebration, either. My husband had been suffering from a nasty back injury for the past few months. Everyone I met had been asking me "How's Niall? How's his back?"

"Well," I replied, "he's in crippling pain but he's in bed. Resting."

"Poor Niall," they say, "How awful."

"Yes," I say. "It is. Awful for him."

But after a couple of months of bringing him cups of tea bed and saying, "How are you, love? Any better today?" The well of sympathy had well and truly run out. "He's in bed," I'd say, "but *I'm* not in bed. *I'm* down here, cleaning the kitchen, writing a book, looking after the kids!"

A few weeks later, frantic with stress from running the show solo, I stood on a rocking chair (!) in my office, propelled myself backwards onto a filing cabinet and cracked a rib. Of course my subconscious must have compelled me to do such a stupid thing in order to get my quota of sympathy. The two of us spent a few hours hobbling around the house, roaring at each other claiming neither of us could lift the baby, until I made a tearful phone call to my mother-in-law who came and did a 48-hour stint and I got two, glorious days in bed.

As a working mother and married woman it seems that all I ever do is moan and nag. I know it's not good but I cannot seem to curb the notion that I have a lot to moan about. And while nagging is a loathsome state of being, the shock and self-loathing I once felt for being a perpetual harridan is gradually wearing off. Nagging works… eventually. Even mild mannered, chirpy married women confess that they do it all the time. I'm always surprised when they tell me I'm "too soft". It seems that as a married woman nagging and moaning have a close correlation with each other. If you nag, things get done and then you have less reason to moan.

Nagging a husband with chronic back pain, however, is not on. So for a while I moaned quite a lot. In my head everything has turned into a source of hardship, even though, really, I still had an enormous amount to be thankful for: my work as a writer, (for which I have the privilege of being published); my weekly column, (which I was lucky enough to have landed during a recession); my adorable baby, (which I gave birth to miraculously at the age of 45); my loyal, supportive husband, whose debilitating injury has made me realise how much he actually does for me and the kids.

While it is perfectly acceptable to ask, "How's the love life?" to single people, nobody ever asks, "How's your marriage these days?" Marriage is supposed to be the end of the line – the happy ending. People are afraid these days of asking in case you say, "I've fallen out of love. We don't talk any more. I'm not getting my 'emotional needs' met," the precursors to so many divorces these days. Thankfully, my husband and I are old fashioned. We have never really "talked" in that mysterious way modern couples are alleged to do. We communicate on a need-to-know basis only – preferring the "less said the better – put up and shut up" school of marital communication to the arduous business of thrashing everything out. We rarely row as a result, which received wisdom also tells us is a 'bad' thing. However, it works for us. If Niall wants to know what I'm feeling he can read my column, and I have learned that men (of which he is the "manly-man" strong silent type – which is why I still fancy him) largely like to figure things out by themselves. Plus I have friends, and children and sisters and a mother to share the vast burden of the bottomless pit of my emotional needs.

As for the feeling of 'being in love'? Please! No marriage can hold the heady collywobbles through the daily passion killers of dirty nappies, dishwasher rotas and nursing a bad back. Anyone who claims it can is faking. The feeling of being in love comes and goes, but it always on hand if you stay grateful for what you've got and stop looking at what's missing.

Twelve years with the same man taught me that true love is not what you feel, it's what you do, including bringing up endless cups of tea-strong, splash of milk, no sugar – and a bit of moaning on the side.

On Working on My Marriage

I'm not very good at taking days off. When I am not working, I am fretting about all the work I have to do. And the only thing that stops me fretting is what I call "recreational work". This is pretend work, usually – who am I kidding – *always* – some inane, pointless activity of a vaguely creative nature that nonetheless satisfies my compulsion to be constantly achieving something. Examples have variously included making jam for the farmers market, hemming curtains, decorating cheap address books with bits of flowery fabric in the mistaken belief that that I will one day store recipes in them in alphabetical order.

Labelling has been a recent obsession. I gave it up a number of years ago when my friend Helen caught me covering a perfectly ordinary jar of coffee in sticky-back gingham and writing "coffee" on the front of it in flouncy handwriting with a black marker. She shamed me into stopping, but I took it up again during a housebound Christmas and have labelled everything in my house, in and out of drawers. OCD highlights include kitchen drawers labelled "tea towels", "baby bibs", "plastic – in use", "plastic – redundant" – right the way down to two small boxes in a bedroom drawer labelled "Kirby grips" and "bobbins". Needless to say both boxes now contain nothing of the sort. There are Kirby grips and bobbins littering the bottom of every handbag and drawer in the house, except for the one I am looking in when I need one.

So, having driven any motivation to clear cupboards out of my system, and my passion for labelling well and truly sated, I decided to spend my day off doing what I always do when I find myself with time on my hands: 'working' on my marriage.

I have always wondered what this meant, and being somebody with a strong work ethic I have chosen to interpret it in a literal sense.

It means sitting down and having a good think about what needs to be "done" in my relationship, then making a room-for-improvement list. I don't think my marriage is so different from anybody else's if I were to admit that the room for improvement list is fairly long and varied. It used to focus on practical things a lot more until a couple of years ago when I was drawing up a housework rotation and realized, to my astonishment, that my husband actually did a lot more housework than me. Now our marriage-work list has the much more ominous task of assessing our emotional status.

At the end of a twelve-month period after losing three close family members and given birth to an unexpected new baby, it probably wasn't a very good idea to go digging around in our mutual psyches.

The phrase "We need to talk" strikes fear into my husband, as it does with many men. So when he came back from the school run I cunningly suggested, "Let's go for a walk."

We loaded up the baby and headed for Belleek Woods. It was a crisp, dry, sunny day and the woods have been cleaned up beautifully, the pathways gritted enough to push a buggy along, but not so much as to make them artificial and park-like.

I kept waiting for the right moment to start with the list. I ran through it in my head. *How are we going to organize our finances? Can we afford a family holiday? What are we going to do about childcare? When are we getting Tom christened?*

To our right the sun glimmered off the River Moy and reflected dappled light through the branches. We had been married in Belleek Castle ten years before, on a stormy day in October, driving down these paths in a horse drawn carriage. Freezing in my flimsy feathery wrap, I remember my limbs buzzing with adrenalin and love, fired up for a future full of warmth and children – certainty at last.

A dog owner passed us and nodded a good morning. I imagined I could feel Niall pleading with me not to destroy our walk with a big talk. *We don't talk any more – we need to go on date nights – when was the last time we went to the pictures – I want to feel more cherished as a woman – I want to know that we're going to be secure – I want guarantees that our children will be properly educated.*

The baby woke up and blew a raspberry. We both laughed.

Why do I need to button everything down with words? Trying to create certainty even – especially – out of the unpredictable. Just leave well alone and enjoy the walk, I thought.

And we both, in our separate ways, breathed a sigh of relief.

On Taking A Walk Down Memory Lane

We were invited to an exhibition opening by our friend Margot at a gallery near Old Street, in London. The work is called *360 days*, and Margot completed a painting every day in 2009 with five days off. I had seen the work on the Internet- a series of small, meticulous canvasses depicting the everyday details of her life for a full year. Margot's work turns the ordinary and domestic into something beautiful and meaningful, and I always find great hope and comfort in it. Plus, it gave Niall and me the perfect excuse for a short break.

Once my heroic sister had offered to take both boys for the weekend, we were set. Niall and I both work from home, so we see more of each other than most couples. While we both have our own work spaces – Niall a boathouse conversion in front of the house, and me a book-lined office – both of us spend ninety per cent of our working lives in our kitchen/living room watching the new baby and working on our laptops. When either of our e-mails pings we say "whose-that?" When Niall had his Dublin design agency he used to commute down every weekend and we barely saw each other. We have gone from living apart most of the week, to being in each other's pockets twenty four hours a day.

The exhibition was a triumph. Sam Taylor Wood opened it and Margot's husband Pat entertained us with his DJ set without stealing the show. It was a warm evening with the London Irish crew turning out in full force and lots of good friends and family rolling in.

At the end of the night everyone moved on to the Hoxton hotel, the centre of a trendy new art area of London, full of galleries and small boutiques and happenings. Fashionable places, be they specific bars or areas of a city, just make me feel tired these days – like I should be wearing something else. Niall and I walked in to the hotel bar and had a quick look around - no seats, loud music – and made an instant, mutual decision to go home.

We took a taxi to Hendon and caught the local fish and chip shop just before it closed and got whatever they had left in the fryer – saveloy, fishcake and chips, doused in salt and vinegar then we sat outside and ate it.

No meal ever tasted as good. Sitting on a shallow brick wall on the edge of a small housing estate in this unremarkable London suburb late on a Friday night reminded me of being young.

"No kids," I said, "it's weird."

"I'd forgotten about them," he said, joking. For a moment it felt like we had just met.

The next day we got the tube across to Notting Hill Gate. Niall moved from Dublin to Notting Hill in the 1980s to live with his older brother, Fintan. Fintan had died the year before, and Niall had an idea to go and find the house they used to live in.

We escaped the mash of shoppers and tourists that snaked from the tube towards Portobello Road. Culchies now, we're not used to the push and shove of city life any more. I gripped onto the back of Niall's jacket and he led me through the crowds like Harrison Ford.

The flat was gone. The whole building had been raised and rebuilt into a Georgian Terrace. Niall was disappointed, but we walked on and found the Windsor Castle, a quirky old pub they used to go to back in the day.

We went in and had a drink, and Niall told me how it had changed. They had opened up the snug, changed the entrance.

I could see them there. Two handsome young Irish men - Fintan a successful graphic designer, his younger brother starting out under his wing, the two lads talking music and trying their luck with the trendy media-type London girls.

Niall and I are husband and wife now, and parents. The everyday makes us dull to each other. Yet our histories – the story of our past, of how we were before we met is as much part of who we are now as the uncut lawns and bin schedules and Lidl trips of today.

We took the tube back to my sister's house in Hendon and I silently remembered the years I spent travelling these tunnels with my own brother, Tom, who also died the year before. Going to parties, punk gigs, drinking, mad teenage messers – he was my best friend.

I reached my hand into the crook of Niall's arm and felt grateful that I was sharing the journey with him. Reaching into the past can be sweet but painful, and it helps if the present looks good.

On Why Hobbies are Better than Spa Weekends

My six-year-old son was watching one of those stations dedicated to men building things with his father. There was a man renovating a VW van and Leo was struck when he announced, "This new engine might have cost me a fortune but this van is my hobby. Without a hobby a man will be unfaithful to his wife…"

Although this sweeping lifestyle statement is not entirely accurate (in my experience many a person has used "gone fishing" as a cover for shenanigans) my son was nonetheless most concerned that my husband and I present to him immediately with our hobbies, presumably to ensure his confidence in the stability of our setup and to prove to him that we are rounded human beings worthy of parenting him.

"Photography," my husband said, a little too quickly. The six-year-old considered him sagely for a moment, then nodded his approval and looked at me.

"Cooking," I said.

"Doesn't count," they both said,

"Emm, reading."

"No, that's work-related . . . and so-," they said quickly before I got the chance to continue, "-does watching television, pointlessly re-arranging things about the house and-," Leo interceded cruelly and loudly, "-going into Penney's to buy stupid knickers!!" - a 'hobby' of mine he particularly despised.

Then it came to me in a flash of brilliance: "Etching," I said. "I did an etching course last year and I thoroughly enjoyed it." Leo was drawing breath to object so I added, "and I'm going to do more of it. Lots more. Every day."

It was a lie. I knew I'd never etch. Not recreationally. Not unless I am in Ballina Arts Centre on a Saturday using it as a legitimate excuse to escape my weekend parenting duties.

Which is terrible because, actually, I do enjoy etching. Far more than I enjoy the other things that eat up my "me" time like going to the gym. I try to make exercise pleasant - I even joined a super-posh gym with a heated pool and a spa.

My entire working day is spent sitting down, writing and eating in equal measure. So in my spare time I feel I should be doing physical exercise. Or at the very least thinking about doing some exercise - an activity which involves sitting in front of the television feeling guilty and one at which I am considerably more proficient at than the exercise itself.

Another problem is that my job, writing, used to be my hobby, and I'm afraid of jinxing my good fortune by committing myself properly to another creative activity. Hobbies distract one from one's work and help one escape from everyday life. Foolishly, I am afraid if I start to enjoy my hobby too much, it will take over my life and I won't want to go back. I am afraid to hobby in case I end up being an etcher full time. Besides, I want my whole life to be recreational and enjoyable - one long hobby.

It's not the physical energy we use in working that has us all stressed and cranky and knackered. It's the constant expectation and craving for success, the pressures of wanting and getting it all. In our frantic, driven, goal orientated, achievement-obsessed society, doing something for the sake of it has never been more important. We are working harder and yet are lazier in the way we recreate. Men watch other men enjoying their hobbies on the TV and women spend a hundred euro on a 'spa-facial' in order to relax, when a spot of etching could do the job cheaper and in my experience, much better.

On My Brother-in-Law's Pasta Machine

I came out of my weekly shop in Lidl and the sun was shining. This was a rare treat, as it is almost always raining in the Ballina Lidl car park. I have come to think of it as a sort of punishment. I go in on a perfect sunny day, get my trolley, fill it – go through my impressive high-speed bagging routine, during which I often attract an audience as I can separate frozen, fresh and larder goods at the same speed the uber-fast checkout workers throw them at me.

I love Lidl. It's cheap, has a limited and regular selection of stock – so you are not loading your trolley with foie gras in a tin and ingredients you are never going to use or forget you already have. (I have about five complete sets of sushi ingredients in my larder and every time I want to make sushi, like, once a year, I go and buy more.)

However my real motivation for shopping there is that I have a weakness for Lidl lifestyle offers. Camping gear, workshop benches, scuba diving equipment, oil-painting kits- wonderful hobby-enabling stuff that inspires me to take up a new activity with impressive Germanic confidence. "Why, if I buy that harness and hat in Lidl, I shall be horse riding in no time!" "A complete set of oils in a box that turns into an easel! Well, if that doesn't get me painting a masterpiece, I don't know what will!"

It is the curse or the gift of a peculiar sort of optimism, depending on how you look at it. If only I had a surfboard, crepe-pan, bread-maker, compost-making kit – everything would be better. Everything could be so different. I'd be the sort of person who'd have crepes for breakfast and go surfing and make-my own compost- whatever that means. It's an escape from oneself, of course, and yet – sometimes it works, and when it does, it's wonderful.

My father-in-law, Joe, who passed away, was my Lidl-buddy. Joe and I clashed horribly at times, but on that one thing we were agreed: Lidl rocked. While my husband and mother-in-law raised their eyebrows in frustration, we formed a sort of Lidl support group. Joe was a generous man and a great man for buying gifts. He was the person who gave Leo his pocket money every week, and he always had the eye out for bargains that he could pass on. The key to Joe's gifts was they had to be something that you didn't know you needed until he arrived up, "da-daah!" and presented you with it. A car cover, hose attachment kit, a pasta-making machine. Most of them went straight into the cupboard with a curt thank-you. Joe didn't mind - he was wiser than that. He knew his stuff would come in handy one day.

And it almost always did. The car cover got dug out and used to cover Niall's vintage jalopy the winter we did the garage up to house his office. A few years later, Niall's brother, Fintan, came home from Australia for my husband's fortieth bash. Big into his food, and something of a gourmet he decided to teach me how to make pasta. Joe's pasta making machine was in the very back of the cupboard under the sink. Covered in that mysterious sticky dust that gets inside my kitchen cupboards, I honesty never thought it would see the light of day. Fintan was thrilled with it and, after a short lesson in making homemade pasta, so was I. It has become one of my kitchen staples, serving all sorts of culinary mood. I use it for kids cooking when the cake icing runs out and if I want to impress guests with homemade ravioli – out it comes.

Since that afternoon when my jovial brother in law broke eggs in my kitchen, and the two of us wondered at the miraculous compulsion of his father to buy me a pasta maker in Lidl, both of those men have died tragically and unexpectedly, insofar as all death is both.

Joe's gifts have outlived him. The car polishing kit is still in the cupboard under the stairs along with the baseball mitt Leo has yet to use. Niall had to fix a burst pipe in the garden the other day and broke open a multi-purpose hose attachment set that has been in the shed for years and which I am certain has Joe's stamp on it.

We took a moment on Leo's communion day to think about his granddad and light a candle for him. We'll continue to miss him on those milestone days with the kids, but it's often in the small details of ordinary life that put us in mind of lost loved ones.

The memories they made for us are the real gifts. I'll never make pasta again without thinking of Fintan and Joe.

On Death

Leo had chosen his Halloween outfit from the vast collection of ghoul masks and pound-shop ensembles he has collected over his eight years. He came downstairs wearing (aside from a scraggy Elvis wig) what seemed like an everyday outfit of sweatshirt and jeans. "That's not much of a costume…" I said. "Da-daa" he announced, lifting up his top to reveal a black vest with skeleton bones on it. "Look," he said laughing delightedly, "I'm really dead!"

At eight years old, Leo knew all about death. That year he had lost two uncles and when he was four his friend, Alana, lost her battle with cancer.

When Alana died, her family waked her at home. She was embalmed and laid out on her regular spot on the sofa in her favourite outfit for two days. It seemed like she was sleeping, plump and pretty, while the network of neighbours and friends who had shared the extraordinary journey of her short, stolen life, milled about eating and drinking and crying.

I didn't know what to do with Leo around it. He was very upset when I told him she had died and when I asked if he wanted to go and see her to say goodbye he said no, he didn't.

The day before the funeral Alana's mother asked if Leo would bring gifts up to the altar. I confessed I was thinking of not bringing him to either the wake or the funeral.

"I'm worried he'll get too emotional," I said. I was not so much worried at his grief, but that his displaying it might upset other mourners. But Una, with her extraordinary strength, reassured me. Death *is* upsetting, she said, let him come and say goodbye.

So I brought him into the house and he saw her and it was fine. Leo was completely composed throughout the funeral Mass while I sobbed horribly and he stroked my face and comforted me.

We got to the graveyard early. I wanted to prepare Leo for the reality of a burial. He ran towards the open grave then came straight back to me full of wonder. "Look, look!" he said, "Come and see!" The grave was lined with wildflowers, a thick mattress of soft, colourful foliage that the men, who had been up the night before digging, had prepared for their neighbour's child. All of the local children were given a flower to throw in on top of their friend. One of them played a traditional air as she was lowered into her new home of flowers.

The day of Alana's funeral was one of the most emotional, but uplifting days I have ever experienced. I will never forget it, and I keep it fresh in my son's mind by talking of her often. We light candles for her after Mass, along with our neighbour's dog Yoda – and now – his two uncles.

The honest, generous way we traditionally handle death is one of the things I most appreciate about being Irish. My reputation as being one of the first on the scene of a recent bereavement is something I get teased about among friends who have lost someone close. If you see me unloading trays of sandwiches and fruitcake out of my jeep, you'll know somebody has died. We say that a good funeral is as enjoyable as a wedding, and while I have yet to attend one that hired a DJ and involved dancing until dawn, there is little doubt that our system for dealing with the emotions that surround the loss of a human life works.

Our traditional culture around death embraces the realities and the strong emotions of early grief. Our fearlessness about displaying our dead loved ones in open coffins, and remembering them with laughter one moment, tears the next, is something we should fight to preserve. I feel saddened when it is increasingly announced in the death notices "house private". While it is every person's choice to grieve as they feel they need to, the snaking lines of mourners outside my local funeral home always impress me. When my brother died in London, although few people here had met him I nonetheless felt supported and strengthened by the good wishes and condolences that came flooding in from my wider community.

Growing up in England, death was an essentially private affair. Funerals were small and closed, and when somebody lost a loved one, we were culturally discouraged from mentioning it. But I have found that when one does take the courage to call and sympathise with an English friend, however reserved they are, there is a palpable sense of relief and a deep gratitude for having made the move. Bluntly, unless you are a member of the royal family, the stiff-upper-lip attitude towards death in England doesn't work. Much better to let it all hang out, like we do.

All Souls Day has become so thoroughly entwined with the children's party atmosphere of Halloween that it is easy to forget it is essentially a time for remembering our dead. Perhaps we have embraced its gaudy commercialism so thoroughly because it acts as a distraction to remembering. Remembering a lost loved one is painful – and it would be sad to think that we are somehow losing the tradition of thoroughly celebrating a person's life through the process of their death. Grief is best experienced as a long and thorough journey. It is emotionally and physically debilitating, and grief gobbles up modern life's most precious commodity – time. My brother died in February and by late Spring I was wondering when I would have the wherewithal to start working properly again.

Life goes on – but being intimately acquainted with death alters life's perspective. It puts mortality at the top of one's list – altering everyday worries like redecorating the house, and pursuing a fulfilling career, and what you are going to wear to a wedding. It causes an adjustment of priorities so that having your hair blow-dried for a function or whether your children brush their teeth or not before they go to bed suddenly seems unimportant. And these things are essential to keep our lives, and the lives of our families, ticking over – so we must try to forget. Forgetting is a necessary way of getting one's own life back. It loosens the painful grip of remembering that the person you loved isn't around anymore, which is why ritual, religious or otherwise, is so important to help ensure we remember.

Keening and waking, month's mind, anniversary Masses and All Souls Day – the rituals that remind us of death are our way of staying honest around – not just death – but life. Talking about who and what we have lost is an important reminder of what we still have. Crucially, honouring our dead on All Souls Day is not just a reminder of what we lost when the person passed, but what we got from them when they were alive. After the first shock of losing someone has passed, going back and remembering who they were, and what they stood for can offer us a valuable opportunity in living our lives to the full. Every time I sit down to write, I remember my brother – a gifted musician – and the way he always encouraged me to be creative. It's still painful, but it's not paralysing like it was before, and pain is not a good enough excuse not to hear Tom's voice in my head.

When my lively, vivacious brother-in-law died in Vietnam, his death was sudden and shocking. Nonetheless e-mails came flooding into my husband's laptop full of warmth and memories of his laughter and easy-going charm. The wound is still raw, but in years to come we will sit around and wonder, "What would Fintan have made of this?"

2009 was a year that brought my family two new babies, as well as lost us two of our precious sons. We will be glad to put it behind us, but we will never forget the two men whose deaths dovetailed into two new lives. Their individuality and the unique gifts that their lives bought while they were in this world will never be allowed slide into infinity.

I remember the day Alana was diagnosed as terminal. Shaken after the news, I was lifting my son out of the bath. Sensing something was wrong he chose the moment to throw a rare tantrum. "I hate you," he screamed, "You're the worst mother in the world!" I held him tight as he wriggled and kicked against my hold – for the first time feeling how strong he was. "He's alive," was all I could think. The words kept repeating themselves back and over like a reel in my head, "He's alive. He's alive." The grip on gratitude I felt in that moment has never left me. Alana's gift will stay with me for as long as I have him. And for that reason, I will always remember her – and so will he.

On the Pressure to Enjoy the Holidays

We had passed the halfway mark of my son's summer holiday, thank God. "Holiday" is a word fraught with the pressure of relaxing and enjoying oneself. Relaxation and enjoyment shouldn't be things that cause stress, but I find that they are.

Firstly, my son's school holiday is three months long. So that's three months during which time I have to ensure his relaxation and enjoyment because the rest of the time the poor, tiny mite has to go to school – an experience which I loathed.

For the first nine years of his life, Leo was a "onesy" (our family name for an "only child", an expression which sounds so lonesome and, in this still-so-Catholic country of ours, smacks of failure). Parents in similar situations know that such children might be easier to feed and house than a gang, but they are harder to occupy.

You can, of course, train them to occupy themselves with television and computers (check), but you are obliged to let them out into the fresh air once in a while and allow them mix with other human beings.

One year I scheduled an intricate childcare rota which involved various summer camps and grandparents when my housekeeper, Theresa, who I was trying to rope into my child-free working summer, pointed out, "It's supposed to be his holiday."

Theresa is great like that – she can always cut straight to the point. A useful talent for when she has to manage the people as well as the house.

That summer had been a successful one for junior. There was a week of outdoor fun on a horse-drawn caravan break straight out of school, then a week watching television and playing Nintendo while Mummy lay prostrate on the sofa recovering. We had great excitement at Nanny Maire's birthday party in Galway, followed by Auntie Sheila and his cousin Lauren coming to stay.

We have a network of fantastic friends so there is rarely a shortage of playmates and my house is familiar with the mayhem of small children running up and down the stairs going "Yeeeee-hoooow!" Small friends occupy him, but they still have to be invited, and fed, and scraped off one another – and in amongst all of this I have to write a book. Because, allegedly, I am a writer who is in the middle of writing a novel, although at the moment it doesn't feel like it. At the moment it feels like I am caught in some awful suspended reality where I should be working, where I want to be working, but I'm not. It's not writer's block. Its summer holiday block, and it happens to me every year.

Every year I am behind when June comes and I decide I have to work hard through the summer to catch up. But writing is such an absorbing activity that I find it impossible with another person – never mind a child – in the house.

When I am working I feel guilty that I am not camping – and when I am camping, I feel guilty that I am not working. I wish I was one of these focused writers who can zone out and switch off from human contact and write with a fierce concentration, but I'm not. There is always a small part of me open to distraction – and there is nothing more distracting than my beautiful son.

Or as Theresa put it when I tutted after he landed in on top of me this morning to give me a no-reason kiss, "It's your summer holiday too, you know."

MANOLOS
(and other style imperatives)

On Shoes

I told my glamorous sister I had flat feet and she responded with the usual complete disinterest in my ailments until I informed her that it meant I could no longer wear high heels.

"What!" she cried.

"That's right, " I said, delighted with the bit of attention. "The physiotherapist told me I can only wear trainers from now on."

"Trainers?" she said, disbelieving.

"With orthopaedic insoles, " I added gravely, "Maximum prescription . . . she said I had the flattest feet she had ever seen." Actually, the physio had let out an involuntary laugh when I walked bare-footed across her consultation room. Involuntary laughter from a health professional is usually a bad sign.

My sister was stricken. Honestly, it was as if I had told her I had cancer. "You're being very blasé about this, " she said, "No high shoes? Ever?"

"That's right, " I said starting to feel a little put out she was getting so het up . . . like it was my fault.

"What will you do if you have to go to a wedding, or a function?"

"I have one pair of black platforms that are ok," I said, realising how pathetic that sounded.

"Well, " she finished, "I don't think you realise how serious this is." She left me sitting in my mother's living room looking at my Nike Air soles, and came back one more time with, "You'll regret it," finally implying that this flat-footedness was somehow a decision that I had come to. A voluntary embracement of sensible shoes, a deliberate attention-seeking veer towards middle age. A premature plea to be taken seriously, like letting your grey grow through in your 30s.

My sister loves shoes. She wears sling-back kitten heels, and she colour co-ordinates them, that sort of thing. I have tried, over the years, to love shoes but I just can't. I always get them wrong.

Even when I could wear high heels I chose cheap high black courts. It seemed a waste trying to match anything else. And then I always get it wrong. I have fat ankles and chunky calves- "upside down legs" my similarly afflicted cousin tells me- so everything strappy makes me look like I'm in drag from the knees down.

The year before I made a final attempt at classy footwear and on the advice of my classy agent went to a posh designer footwear emporium where a coiffed sales assistant pressured me into splurging a horrific amount of money on a pair of red brogues. Tragically, they do not fit my 'special' insoles and so sit in their posh fabric shoe bag glowering up mournfully every morning at me like a couple of needy puppies. I bloody hate them.

It seems to me that the world truly is divided into women who love shoes and women who are indifferent to them. Women who love shoes wear Jimmy Choo and crave Manolo Blahnik, while indifferent women wear whatever they can pick up - that looks vaguely passable with what they are wearing - from any shop that sells them for less than 50 euro. Indifferent women often end up like me, tortured after years of wearing cheap plastic stilettos and crappy supermarket trainers, in old-lady comfortable lace-ups before their time.

The thing is, I keep trying to bring myself to care, but I can't. It's a relief actually. It's one less decision to make in the mornings. And yet despite my innate indifference I still fear I may be missing out. Imagine. The world is so consumer driven that I feel pressure to want to want shoes. Now that's what you call a 'middle class problem'.

KATE KERRIGAN

On Wanting A Posh Spice Bob

Celebrities: big-haired, orange-skinned, glittery toothed, balloon-breasted, bubbly clones with obviously made-up names like "Jade" and "Jordan". Who in their right mind would want to emulate these modern monstrosities?

And yet surely the most offensive thing about these people is the insidious way they creep into your subconscious so that even when you do not care in the least about any of them - you find that, in actual fact, you do. We are so saturated with celebrity culture that it is no longer enough to simply not care. For instance, I do not care about "Posh Spice". See? I even write her name in quotation marks to illustrate the extent of my aloof, superior disinterest. And yet two weeks ago I sat in front of my hairdresser and asked for a bob. "With long bits at the front - you know - like. . ." And there it was. I wanted a Posh Spice haircut. Did knowing that deter me?

No. Because despite my better judgment my little celebrity gremlin was whispering: "Posh Spice has a bob - bob *gooood haircut.*"

Ditto teeth whitening. My dentist has been badgering me to have my teeth whitened for ages. Last year I almost had an excuse to travel to Los Angeles and she lost the run of herself altogether insisting that I could not travel to the west coast of America with "ordinary" teeth with the urgency more suited to an emergency root canal. Eventually I gave in, but deep inside I knew it was not her insistence that got to me. It was the pearly-white gnashers gleaming from the stack of *Hello!* magazines in her waiting room.

Gradually, after years of fillings and drillings, I decided - dammit - I want teeth like Paul McCartney, and Billie Piper and the woman who won herself a job working for that angry looking man who does the ads for Prize Bonds. As I was leaving her surgery with several hundred pounds worth of tooth-bleach and my set of see-through inverted dentures, she informed me I wasn't to drink anything that would stain, especially tea or coffee, for a fortnight. I am completely dependent on both - yet I did manage to salvage comfort from reassuring myself that, in all probability, Eva Longoria was also going to bed that night with her mouth crammed full of bleach and plastic.

And then I thought, this is how it begins. This is how a normal woman starts to morph herself into a footballer's wife for no better reason than she can. All it takes is hard work (the gym), courage (Brazilian wax), creativity (skilled application of make-up), endurance (the constant diet), a sense of humour (spray tan), money (a designer wardrobe) and a surgeon for everything else. What it does not take a great deal of is brains. So while there are people we admire greatly for their wit and intellect, sadly few of us aspire to look like true idols such as Alan Bennett, Germaine Greer, Vincent Browne or Melvyn Bragg (except, his smile suggests, Melvyn Bragg himself). There was no greater illustration of this than the great film director Ken Russell's brief sojourn in the *Big Brother* house. (I can't help it. It's an addiction).

I'm afraid of where it might lead. Teeth bleaching is the middle ground in commitment vanity, coming somewhere between the ability to apply mascara in a moving vehicle and hard-core liposuction. Should I get my forehead injected with Botox? Or perhaps I'll get my bob readjusted to incorporate a fringe instead to make me look like Juliette Binoche. She's a French celeb; that's got to be posher than "Posh".

On Trying to Look Like Kate Moss

I tried to drum up a bit of interest in the Kate Moss line at Topshop, but just couldn't whisker up enough of myself to give a shite. I think that's personal progress, especially for a woman who, at 40-plus, owns a Madonna at H&M chav-tastic tracksuit.

Armed security were on the doors of Topshop branches in central London (well, not armed, but certainly very serious looking), along with riot police on stand-by, that sort of thing. When the first Primark (Penneys) shop opened in London's Oxford Circus people camped outside overnight and the police were called several times to separate women who were fist fighting in order to get their hands on sequinned mini-dresses for £10.99.

The day after Kate's groundbreaking collection arrived in-store I heard some hapless PR on the radio trying to justify the hysteria by explaining: "Girls can walk in here and buy a waistcoat, a pair of shorts and some ankle boots and then -" Then what? Climb Mount Everest? Wrestle Brad from Angie? Run for US presidential election? "- they are dressed just like Kate!"

It is not disaffected youth or bad politicians that are most likely to elicit the cliché "What is the world coming to?" but women shopping.

So here it is once and for all. If you go into a popular high-street store and spend a few hundred euro on half-sewn, dodgy-seamed clothing doubtless made by poverty-stricken labour in a third-world country it will not, ever, under any circumstances, help you look like Kate Moss or Madonna. Ever.

I know this because I have tried it and it doesn't work. Buying clothes because they look nice on famous people, or because you saw them in a magazine, or because they are really, really cheap is stupid.

When I say it like that I know it's true; however I am still unable to control the homing device in my brain which guides me into a branch of Penneys on an almost daily basis to buy legwarmers I don't need and miniature lingerie which chafes . . . I am hopeful that my Madonna tracksuit (ruched at the bust, nylon, sparks in the dark) may have cured me.

My husband finally made me put the jacket in the bin last week. I am allowed to wear the bottoms with a plain sweater on top but the double ensemble is gone.

So in it went to the St. Vincent de Paul bin-bag mountain that is my conscience alleviator. Then I heard a lovely posh woman on the BBC say this week that all this cheap crappy clothing that we chuck in the recycling bin is worse than useless. Much of it ends up as landfill, as it is such poor quality and so badly made that it can't be sold in the shops of the developing countries it goes to.

If we bought fewer, properly made clothes, poor people would benefit more. For the same reason developing nations are insulted by our sending them our out-of-date processed leftover food, they also do not appreciate our 'two for the price of one' high-fashion tatty cast-offs . . . even if they come with the labels still on.

The chances are if you're not going to wear a faulty lemon-yellow boob tube, neither is anyone else, no matter how poor they are.

So before you drop that nasty fashion mistake in the charity collection bag . . . think on. Perhaps it would be better used for stuffing a cushion? Or better again, don't bloody buy it in the first place.

On What To Wear

The more I travel, the less I like it and the more neurotic I become about leaving home.

When I am in the middle of a book, life, by necessity, is all about comfort and focusing my mind on my work. Most days, I draw a pair of sweat pants on over my pyjamas and, dropping the baby off at the childminders on the way, retreat to my mother's shed where I hide out, drinking coffee, eating biscuits and trying to concentrate on my book until it is time to haul my head back out into the "real world" of shopping, cooking and watching TV with my family.

My three boys and my mother are just about all I can manage in the way of human contact on any given day. Everyone else is accessed by telephone or e-mail so they cannot see how appallingly groomed I am. I fantasise that this is a temporary state, but as books pile up and the years and weight pile on, I fear this self-contained lump of knitwear glaring at the computer is the real me.

Into all of this came an invitation to a big awards ceremony in London.

It wasn't for another two weeks but I was already consumed with it. I reflected on a time when I really loved this aspect of my life. Cosily working away in solitude, then having to hop on a plane and go off and be all glamorous and glittery and bask in the glory of being a published novelist for a couple of days before I come home to be taken for granted as scruffy old mum and wife. It was my version of "me" time – publishers fussing over me, using a city trip as an excuse to get in a bit of shopping and lunch with girlfriends who miss me and tell me I'm great – and all with the excuse of work so I can hold my moral high-ground at home and pretend that I am not enjoying myself when, in actual fact, I am.

Somewhere, in my contentment with my life in Killala, this infatuation with my own glamour disappeared.

Once I booked the flights and the hotel, I had to find something to wear. This is one of the aspects of my life that I have grown to hate. My job either requires me to wear comfortable clothes that nobody sees (a cacophony of whatever is closest to hand and will fit over my pyjamas from mine, my husband's or mother's wardrobe) or full on TV-friendly eveningwear. There is nothing in-between. No smart daywear, or little business suits required. Upon inspection, not one of my evening dresses fit me, apart from a black, stretchy Ghost dress I bought to carry me through my first pregnancy ten years before and which is so worn I had taken to wearing as a nightie. So it was either that with some kind of a spangly wrap or cardigan to cover my disgraceful arms, or my 'old faithful' black designer dress. However, I could not do the straining zip up without the help of my husband (who wasn't coming) and which, in any case, would require an industrial strength girdle (which I was woefully out of the habit of wearing), and another, longer confection to hide the arms and the gaping back.

For the life of me I couldn't drum up one iota of enthusiasm for buying a new frock. I had a long and very boring conversation with my sister about it. Being ten years younger than me, she still cares about such things. We went through her entire wardrobe and decided that anything she had would make me look like Kat out of *Eastenders* – a look I had gone for in the past, but just didn't have the va-va-voom in me to carry off any more.

"Monsoon in Galway will have something that fits you," she said. "I'll take the afternoon off – it'll be fun!"

"No," I said, "I can't face it."

In the end, I decided to go the easy route and re-instate my Ghost nightie as a dress and apply myself to sourcing a sequined cardigan – fingers crossed for the Dunne's Christmas collection. I packed my rollers, piled my hair up and stuck in some class of a mad fascinator to distract attention from the scruffy hem and high shoes, which, at a recent book launch, I estimated were two years older than my publicist.

I headed off in my track suit with my glamorous alter ego packed into a wheelie suitcase, and started my trek towards the bright-lights of a big city, where I would network, and charm, and stay out so late that I didn't have time to miss my three beautiful boys and my charmed, cosy life in Ireland.

On Labels

What's with all the labels? They were talking on the radio about Yummy Mummies and Slummy Mummies and Alpha Mums. Or perhaps you're a Rock Chick or a Glamorous Granny or a Frock Jock (Female DJ… wake up at the back!). I mean, how boring is it? They don't have the same for men. Men are just "blokes" or "guys" or, if you want to push the boat out, "complete bastards". Oh no- wait a minute- what about the New Man, the House Husband or… as one journalist recently helpfully invented, Gay Dad? You see, this is the problem. This is why women are still doing the lion's share.

Women have sassy aspirational labels cunningly designed to make us spend money on designer accessories, lose weight and wear sexy get ups while wheeling the Mama's & Papa's three-wheeled buggy around Sundrive Superquinn hunting for Nigella-inspired ingredients to turn us into Domestic Goddesses. Men's lifestyle labels are just basically terms of abuse. House Husband and New Man, however much we might have been relieved by them, are just basically male code for a whipped man-slave or Big Girl's Blouse.

Horribly, in my early, impressionable 20s I became enthralled and infatuated with the lone male journalist on *Cosmopolitan* magazine, who was the individual actually responsible for creating the phrase "New Man" in the late '80s, thus launching a generation of sensitive, caring men not afraid to show their feelings. Several years later, having relieved almost every female journalist in London of her propriety (and thanks to a boastful nature, their dignity too) this man finally confessed to me that being Mr. Sensitive and Caring New Man was actually just a quick, cheap route to get a woman into bed. Thankfully the *Loaded* men's magazine culture put a stop to that in the '90s and men reverted back to Neanderthal form, where at least we women knew where we were with them again.

Which is more than we can say for where we are with ourselves. Seemingly Yummy Mummies are "out". So having tortured ourselves with highlights, vaginal depilation, fake tan, tits and nails to fit the brief, we are now told "Yummies" are scrounging ladies-who-lunch and what we have to do is become Alpha Mummies. In other words all of the above whilst running Citibank and chairing an international charity. Men's modern-media labels on the other hand merely encourage them to remain beer swilling, chest-beating 14-year-old fart monsters. It's a conspiracy. It has to be. We get lured into labelling it as a 'bit of fun'. But actually, it isn't fun at all.

I frequently have a 'morning-matching-moment' where I feel it would be just letting the side down to turn up at my son's school at 9am looking under par, i.e. in my natural state. So at three minutes to nine I am stressed trying to figure out what to wear because some mother, who has already seen me looking like dog-food at least 30 times already this month, might label me 'slummy' instead of 'yummy'. And I live in rural Mayo where such labels don't exist except in the heads of a few impressionable media junkies (like me, obviously). I am so tired of living up to my own interpretation of these stupid labels, but perfectionism, even (especially) when you fall so far short of it, is addictive.

On the other hand I guess there is nothing more annoying than perfection in a person. That's my excuse anyway.

On 'Sex and the City'

I was on my way for a weekend away and on the car journey to the airport I tuned to Derek Mooney who, to my absolute delight, promised me that, after the news, I would be treated to Dermot O'Neill talking about bedding plants. I positively bristled with joy. I know it is the onset of middle age, but that is just exactly the kind of radio programme I like to listen to when I am "off" work. Pop music reminds me that I should be doing a workout, and people ringing up and giving out about everything and anything from the HSE to people picking their noses on public transport either sends me into an emotional decline or makes me want to 'talk to Joe' in an enraged frenzy of indignation.

Bedding plants was about all I was fit for. "But first, "Mooney announced "the big final of our Mooney/Sunday World 'Sex and the City' Quiz."

What followed was a "battle royale" as various teams of people calling themselves the Limerick Ladies, Sligo Sirens and the Donegal Dolls quizzed it out to win a holiday to New York, marking the history-making release on the big screen of 'Sex and the City'.

I have never felt like such a boring killjoy in my entire life. "Oh NOOOOO!" I cried (while my husband, who is one of those extraordinary people who absorbs television trivia by osmosis gamely guessed the correct name of Charlotte's mother-in-law), "Bring me back my bedding plants!"

I like 'Sex and the City', and frequently find myself flicking to the endless re-runs on Sky. It's the kind of programme you can watch again and again because the plot is always so shallow and meaningless that you've forgotten what happened when you last watched this episode not a fortnight beforehand. It is decorative, enjoyable pap.

Yes, the clothes are lovely and I love lovely clothes. I knew that if I went and saw the film I would probably enjoy it. It is not outside the bounds of possibility that, as a result of watching the film, for a few days I will be vaguely influenced by it and possibly even dig out a matching shoes and handbag combo for my supermarket run. It is also, predictably, annoyingly likely that I will come away from it and crave its silly glamour over the practical judgment I covet for myself.

However, what I cannot fathom is the way it has permeated female culture and our relentless celebration of a programme which holds up a picture of womanhood which is, essentially, shallow and morally dubious - telling us that buying loads of pairs of expensive shoes and having mountains of casual sex are female achievements. Time and again in the run-up to this movie, I was asked if I was a Carrie, Samantha, Miranda or Charlotte. As if every type of woman were identified here. As far as I can see, the choice is neurotic, slut, workaholic or anal-retentive - all fine as long as you are wearing fabulous accessories.

There is something about that programme that brings out the curmudgeonly old feminist in me. It seems to me that this 'Sex and the City' cult was fashioned out of a flimsy novel into a cultural phenomenon by cynical marketing men who presented a warped view of modern womanhood and seduced us into embracing it by dangling glittery accessories in front of our eyes.

Is there not a middle ground between it and 1980s prisoner-of-war drama 'Tenko'? And if there is, can we find it before I take somebody's eye out with my Manolo?

On Being Satisfied With Who You Are and Just Getting On With It.

"New Year, New You!" This is the year you get to be a slimmer, fitter, lovelier, version of "you". All you have to do is apply yourself properly this year and you could really turn things around and change from being the failed miserable person you are now to a happy, shiny person you have always wanted to be. You know, that drink/smoke-free, fresh-faced person with no points on their licence and a tidy cutlery drawer! So throw out that wardrobe, give up carbs, change the car, your hair colour, and redecorate the house.

In fact, instead of just fecking around trying to lose those final five pounds and upgrading your bedroom curtains, why not go the whole hog and dispense with "you" altogether? Take on an alternate identity . . . maybe you could sell the house and use the money for major surgery? Then you could move to another country, ditch your partner, put your children into foster care . . . and create a brand new history for yourself.

The whole New Year resolutions thing is the most ghastly illustration of how far we have not come as human beings. In the wake of Christmas where we have spent an average of 1,500 euro on mindless crap per household, we are now going to pronounce that the mince pies, the brandy, the Quality Street vegetation in front of six-hour TV-watching marathons, was a slothful, sinful waste of time and try to punish ourselves for it in the New Year.

We enjoy ourselves by over-indulging then we punish ourselves. What a stupid way to live.

Why are we never ever happy with what we have got? Is it just a construct or are we human beings just naturally programmed to dissatisfaction: to always want to be thinner, richer... have a bigger car, bigger bosom, a bigger, better house?

Let's break the mould and this year and say: "This year I am just going to bloody well get on with it and stop moaning about my kids, the car, the spouse." Or even: "Hurray! I am still alive! I ate this many carbs, smoked this many fags, went this far over my recommended alcohol limit, had this much drunken unprotected sex and yet . . . here I still am for another year!"

Make this year the year you become a marginally less postmodern neurotic. Now that's something worth aiming for.

KATE KERRIGAN

On Putting One's Cleavage Into Retirement

Someone once accused me of being a prude because I wore a high-necked blouse to a book launch. Winter was approaching and it was nippy. I didn't really think about it until a gang of my chums gathered to reprimand me for being dressed like Supernanny and bemoaned my lack of cleavage. It wasn't that I had deteriorated so badly that I needed a licence to wear a low-cut dress, it was just that I couldn't see the point any more. It just hit me one night as I was rummaging for a lacy vest to modify a particularly plunging neckline . . . what's the point in cleavage? It's winter, it's getting colder, so what purpose does cleavage serve really apart from giving men the idea that they might want to have sex with me? None that I could particularly think of . . . and as I already have a husband who I can have sex with any time I want, I thought perhaps I should just gradually retire them from the public eye.

However, it seems that my aspiration to cover up is bizarre, certainly if the social pages are anything to go by. Celebrities, most especially of the reality television variety, seem to make a very good living out of it. Some of us write columns, nurse dying people, and teach children for a living. Others have job descriptions that read "Go about in a bikini". Fair enough. Showing off in their knickers is how they feed their families and keep themselves in skimpy frocks.

What I cannot understand is how professional, intelligent women have allowed themselves to be drawn into this alarmingly antifeminist theory that displaying a pair of bouncy breasts in a string top is somehow sexually liberating.

Just who exactly is being sexually liberated here? Is it the fortysomething public relations executive letting it all hang out in a leopard print Versace hanky/dress at Punchestown? Or is it the teenage boy who has discovered there's more porn to be had in some of his mum's society magazines than the top shelf 'tut-tut' material. By all means, young single women, knock yourselves out. Get on the glitter and the glamour and get out there and compete. But wives at charity functions, mums at school fetes and the 40-plus female market in general, let's all try and get a grip on this pressure to expose ourselves. Let's just be honest with ourselves and accept that there comes a time when an older lady must retire her bits and bobs and file them away behind a nice blouse and a bit of classy tailoring.

There will be black tie balls when the call of the once-magnificent cleavage may be answered but please, invest in a chiffon shrug.

Because there is no amount of buffing, and bronzing, polishing or pruning that will disguise a billowing bingo wing or, that most unfortunate phenomenon, the five-pronged armpit wrinkle. I'm not advocating full burqa, although I am not entirely averse to the idea.

On a trip to Morocco a few years ago, I tried dressing myself neck to ankle in black. I found great freedom in being able to interview and communicate nicely with the local men. It is not that Arab men leer more than Irish men, they are just more open about it. Arab men also believe that if you show them your breasts, even a bit of them, it is because you want them to leer at you. Irish men leer behind our backs, sputtering into their pints in corners. Local men also understand this insane western rule we have that it's okay to show the whole breast apart from the nipple. The nipple is pornographic, but all the rest of the breast is fine. Our own men also generously go along with our pretence that excessive cleavage is either a fashion-statement or caused by the 'accidental' droop of an ill-fitting top.

There is a saying that if a western woman gets caught naked she covers her breasts and her groin with her hands. An Arab woman covers her face, because your face is what identifies you as an individual. It is the most significant part of us because it is our tool for communicating, the place that illustrates our personality. Older women should have the confidence to use it to attract and maintain interest from men, women, and colleagues without needing the distraction of great tracts of bare flesh.

I've dusted off my black polo necks, but then it's easy with winter drawing in to get judgmental about bare chests. Come spring, I'll probably be out frightening workmen in a halter neck top again.

On What's In and What's Out

I can't cope with In/Out lists. I'm too impressionable and tend to read them as rules, weekly instructions for living. They used to just put them in women's fashion magazines but now they are in every newspaper supplement and this gives them an importance that unnerves me.

There is bad stuff going down everywhere in the world right now, our children are obese and by the way, footless tights are OUT but leggings are back IN.

Is life not complicated and difficult enough without having to worry about what things are fashionable or unfashionable?

Shall I use balsamic vinegar in my salad dressing or is it 'Down'. Is cider vinegar 'Up' this week or did I just read something about it being good for arthritis in a health column's 'Do' box?

Reminds me of my magazine editing days when my sister was comforting me over a headline that I allowed to go to print with an instruction to 'Put Headline Here'. She told me of a 'Do! Don't!' column which once appeared in a large, reputable British women's magazine. The yellow and red box was filled with the words 'Please write any old s*** here, please write any old s*** here'. It was cheering to know that other, better-paid people were as bad at their jobs as I was.

Do/Don't lists are not important, and in fairness to the people who write them they are not intended to be taken as such, but knowing this does not stop me from allowing them to feed my low-level could-do-better anxiety. There are people capable of taking no notice of such fripperies, but sadly I am not one of them. I say I am, I think I am and then... BAM!... I am standing at the tights section of Dunne's musing over a pair of legwarmers or turning my nose up at goat's cheese because it's 'passé', then panicking because maybe it was 'passé' before and now it's 'Back In!'

It's not like I am completely neurotic or have nothing better to do. I have loads of very important stuff to do and consider myself a reasonably lackadaisical, tolerant type. It's just that I am drawn to the type of recreational media material that makes me feel guilty.

I always just said I wasn't interested in gardening, but when they started to put gardening programmes on prime-time television that all changed and I became a failed gardener. One of these pathetic people who would love to have a nice garden but is too lazy and stupid to go out and gets their hands dirty. Rather like those laughable idiots who are still using balsamic vinegar in their salad dressing, or gauche females who have neglected to trade in their opaque tights for patterned ones.

Interiors programmes are the worst, bringing years of blood, sweat and tears tumbling down as you watch somebody transform their shabby living room into a lounge in the Four Seasons with two bits of re-cycled foam and a tin of Dulux they found in the shed.

On a bad day, even real news and documentaries make me feel guilty. I shouldn't be sitting here watching/reading this. I should be in Darfur/Soweto feeding refugees/building houses. Travel supplements- they have to go straight in the bin. I've seen nothing of the world... been nowhere! Arts- when was the last time I went to the theatre? I'm a complete philistine.

By far the worst are these prescribed parenting programs.

These are the only programmes that make me feel so guilty they propel me into actual action. My poor sons don't know whether they're coming or going with star charts and naughty steps all implemented in a half-hearted only-makes-things worse kind of way. I don't have especially low self-worth but there is a corner of my psyche that is obviously lacking, and it is into this corner that the media seems able to frenzily feed. Alcohol is grand stuff, but in the hands of an alcoholic it becomes deadly. Ditto Do/Don't lists to the slightly insecure and gardening programmes to the foolishly ambitious. They're not supposed to make you feel stupid and bad, but they do.

Of course, there is a fix. *Big Brother* and/or *Hello!* magazine.

The best way to dig yourself out of the media guilt pit is to trade down. Bad and all as I am at least I've not resorted to reality television/plastic surgery.

On Being a Happy Old Hag

I have discovered a fabulous new anti-ageing trick. It involves removing half of the mirrors in my house.

It was inspired by one of those annoying skin-cream ads on the TV at featuring Claudia Schiffer talking about what a struggle it is getting older. She actually uses the word "heal" – the implication being that if you are getting older you are ill in some way. Wrinkles are called "damage" in this new world where women must fight, fight, fight against getting older. Ageing is the new disease. It has to be cured, or "reversed" and, at all costs, made to go away.

If there is one thing that you can be sure is going to happen to you in your life it is this: you *will* get older. Then, at some point down the line, you will die. That's the *only* certainty there is.

So, as if my life wasn't hard enough – with kids and work and having to have a perfect house, and a perfect wardrobe and enough groom time to keep my highlights up to speed – I have to actually defy nature and not get old. Or at least hide the process from the outside world with every bit of energy I can muster.

I became particularly sensitive about this subject when I realised, very suddenly, that I somewhere along the line I had crossed some kind of threshold visa-vi my physical appearance.

I do try not to be overly neurotic about what God gave me. I would like to be slimmer and brave enough to wax, but you can't have everything. I have achieved a certain level of laissez fair about my looks – or lack of them – because I had always been able to rely on an ability to put myself through hair and make-up and come out transformed at the other end. I could happily push myself forward into the public eye knowing that once I had whacked on the slap and thrown in a few heated rollers I would come out the other end looking fresh and groomed and ready for my cocktail – if not my close-up.

However, the last few times I had gone out, there had been a point in the evening where I had caught sight of myself in a mirror and gone, "Rah! Who's that?!"

I have never gone in for the no-make-up-make-up look. As far as I am concerned if you are going to go to all that effort, you might as well go the whole hog. But as a woman who had been sauntering through her forties, happy and confident – I had suddenly hit the brick wall of looking like somebody I don't recognize. When, exactly, did I become a middle-aged woman in too much make-up? Or a jowly bag lady? There didn't appear to be any middle ground. When I am not made up, I look like my brother in a wig. When I make an effort I just seem to look like mutton dressed as lamb. When I tone down the cleavage and the big hair and the smoky eyes and the glitter, I look tweedy and old, like Angela Lansbury.

I suppose the real truth is that I'm fighting against glamour more and more as I get older. I am a sensible old-lady novelist trapped in a Joan Collins make-up routine. I want to be Angela Lansbury. I want to wear high-waist beige slacks, and nice blouses and tweed jackets and have my hair blow-dried into a solid "do" and take my lipstick out of my bag in taxis, slick it and pucker it without looking in the mirror. I want to be slightly portly, and rather clever, and have young people defer to me in a mystery-solving, amused but respectful way. I want to be my favourite aunt, and wear smart-casual jeans to prune my garden, and sensible shoes, even when I am out and clip a nice broach onto my lapel and go for lunch in hotels and shrug my shoulders and say, "This is lovely."

What I do not want to do is have to go to the gym every day and slather myself day and night in serums to try and make myself look twenty years younger than I am so I can go out late at night because I am the new breed of "cougar".

When did female role models for women of my age become such hard work and, frankly, so undignified? Can we still look up to Madonna? Now there's that ghastly U.S. drama *Cougar Town* where Courtney Cox and her cohorts go around clambering over teenage boys. Looking and acting your age has become synonymous with "Letting Yourself Go" when it should be "Copping Yourself On".

Getting older should be an invitation to embrace dignity, wisdom and the experience of a life full of adventure and education.

I, for one, have started digging out my Miss Marple pearls and twin-set for the spring.

On Why I Wish Madonna Would Chill Out

I'm one of a generation of women who have been influenced all my adult life by Madonna. Some years ago, somebody wrote a book called *I Dream of Madonna*, cataloguing the dreams average women of my generation have had about the pop idol. She captured our imaginations with fishnets, footless tights, floppy lace hair bows and atrocious pop-songs, but has ended up residing so thoroughly in our collective subconscious that I do, in fact, regularly dream of hooking up with Madge in various locations (nightclubs, Tesco, the Brown Thomas car park) and becoming her best friend.

I'm not a particular fan of her music – I'd never pay to actually see her in concert or anything like that – and although I thought her last album was rather good, it was, frankly, a bit of a surprise. But despite that, I have always had an interest in the way she conducted her life.

I saw *In Bed With Madonna* in the cinema, and thoroughly enjoyed the programme on the telly when she was floating about doing good works for her cult, and when it showed her sitting about, bored, in the pub waiting for her slobbery husband to finish his pint, then gave out about him saying that marriage was a big fat disappointment but you just had to get on with it. I loved that.

There is something so comforting about so much of what Madonna says. When someone you think is marvellous says, "Everyone probably thinks that I'm a raving nymphomaniac, that I have an insatiable sexual appetite, when the truth is I'd rather read a book," you think, me too! It's not much, it's not important, but in its own little way it helps.

When she was younger, Madonna's attitude was, "I'm tough, I'm ambitious and I know exactly what I want. If that makes me a bitch, okay" – and while it's not very nice, on some crude level it's admirable. Deep down, in an embarrassed corner of myself, I have always wanted to be Madonna. Until recently. Because now Madonna is nearly 50 and she is appearing on the front cover of women's magazines in hotpants. Does she look undignified? No. Is it inherently wrong for women of a certain age to bomb about dancing to loud disco music? No. But is it something that I personally aspire to? No, it is not.

I suppose I should, but when I see Madonna now- thighs like steel, coiffed hair, muscular arms- I just think, "God, woman, when are you going to give it up!" I read interviews where she confesses she spends two hours working out each day. Ashtanga yoga, world tours, arduous work schedules – when I was younger all that seemed exciting, like something to aspire to. Nearing my mid-40s, it seems like too much hard work.

I wish my idol would just take it a bit easier. Put on a few pounds, complain publicly about her impending arthritis, be seen in Burger King with the kids eating their leftover nuggets, saying, "Sod it, I'm nearly fifty, time to relax," and give her acolytes something more manageable to aspire to. Because, frankly, I'm a bit knackered with it all already.

The thought that I might still be dieting, exfoliating, and craving to be more successful, richer, wiser and more beautiful into my 50s is, honestly, just too awful a fate to contemplate. I wish she'd just chill out, and give the rest of us aging, hard-nosed '80s goddesses permission to do the same.

On the Perfect Blouse

I was getting ready for a speaking engagement and instead of just admitting I was nervous, I got myself into a state and decided that I had nothing to wear. I had black trousers and jacket but what I had was no blouse.

"I have no blouse," I said to myself, whilst fingering and flicking aside at least six of them. What I meant was, "I have no blouse which will make me feel better about myself. No blouse that will lift my spirit and make my nerves go away and make me look to other people as if I am a serious person who is cleverer than I actually am. Yes, I have blouses, but I have no blouse that actually suits me." The reason for this (and you would think that having been dressing myself for 40-odd years I might have spotted it by now) is that blouses do not suit me.

However, this fact had not halted my ongoing grá for the sexy-secretary look, the pencil skirt with pussy-bow collar worn in a post-modern ironic way. Every season it comes back and every season (despite the fact that I have abnormal feet and cannot wear high heels and therefore pencil skirts) I decide that blouses are 'the thing'. However, blouses do not make me look like a sexy secretary. They make me look like a middle-aged woman in a blouse. For pussy bow blouses to be sexy they have to be worn by 18-year-old old fashion models. Otherwise you're in Angela Lansbury/Miss Marple territory.

None of this entered by conscious mind, unfortunately, before I made it into a Top Shop.

Imagine my joy when I found not an ordinary blouse, but a "directional top". It had cropped frilly sleeves, a high neck and a slit down the back. I could barely contain my excitement when I looked at myself in the dressing room mirror.

This was it! Directional, great with jeans, funky . . . I had, at last, deservingly found my blouse. So I bought four- one in every colour. It cost me 125 euro but, as I said to my underwhelmed husband when I got home and ripped open the bag, "I won't need to buy another thing this winter. This," I announced, holding the frock/smock/blouse confection aloft, "is 'Kate… Autumn/Winter 2007'. This will carry me day-into-evening, casual-to-smart. This is all I need."

Two days later I decided I was ready to present 'Kate… Autumn/Winter 2007' to the public. As you can imagine, people were lining the streets…not. Except that when I actually put my miracle blouson on it turned out to be an absolute monstrosity. It looked beyond ridiculous. Instead of looking like a middle-aged woman in a blouse, now I looked like a middle-aged woman in a horrible blouse. Worse again, I realised that where my fashion mistakes once were an unfortunate mishap one could overlook, they now look almost comical.

I did give my blouson top a single outing, to a business meeting with my writing partner who is so utterly uninterested in clothes that she wouldn't notice if I turned up in a bikini.

"How do you like my blouse?" I asked.

"It's very frilly, " she said . . . far, far too quickly.

When are they going to start putting security guards at the door of Topshop to stop old people like me getting in and buying things which are too young for us? Is it wrong to grieve that I have moved a fashion season closer to the 'smart-casual/tailored-separates' phase of my life?

On Watching Your Weight

I have always loathed gyms, and I can trace some of the most stressful and miserable hours of my life to the soulless interior of one particularly large and expensive south Co Dublin outfit which I joined to rid myself of the extra two stone I gained carrying my first son. One day while I was in there for a rare outing with my husband – justifying our €2,000 family membership which I horribly calculated to work out at €100-per-swim – I met a posh blonde snobby woman I knew.

"I'm one of those nouveau housewife clichés I'm always laughing at!" I wailed afterwards. "Nonsense," he said until I laid the five points of evidence, finger by finger, in front of him. "I know her, I have highlights, I drive a jeep, we live in Harold's Cross and we're in here!"

Spiritually, I think I moved to Mayo at that moment.

And in my new home, I have found a way to get in shape while avoiding thin women with Brazilians or – God forbid – men who, generally I feel, have no place in the business of helping me dispose of my unwanted fat.

First stop was Weight Watchers – or Biscuits Anonymous, as I like to call it. Our leader Ann had the somewhat intimidating talent of remembering the name of every woman who has ever been to her Weight Watchers group and greets me each time I go back as if I have never been away. This has the positive effect of making me feel not like a complete failure, which in terms of being a committed weight-watcher I most certainly am.

Ann favours the group therapy approach and gets us to share tips and progress with one another, picking us off, pound by pound after our weigh-in. She also has the uncanny talent of remembering our anecdotes – like the one I related when I was in my all-too-brief I-enjoy-exercise phase, using it against me when I'm having an attack of self-cynicism which, let's face it, is most weeks.

Having said that, I now sit for the full half-hour meeting gradually resigning myself to the fact that the only way I am going to retain any semblance of control over my sugar habit is by returning here, every Wednesday, for the rest of my life. Which, amazingly, doesn't seem like too terrible a prospect.

Next up was Aqua Gym. This I call Oestrogen Soup – for this is what you will find in the Ballina municipal pool on a Monday and Wednesday night. Thirty or forty women of all shapes, sizes, ages and levels of physical fitness pile into the heavily chlorinated, barely tepid water and pound and jog and turbo swim to the instructions of Orla – whose tiny frame belies a hefty voice that determinedly hollers us all into shape.

There are no Molton Brown shower gel dispensers here. It's a scrum for the post-swim hose-down, lots of sharing shampoos and queuing – but I don't go there for the "spa". I go there because there is no competition, no checking out of each other's swimwear, no need to epilate or pedicure or any of that stressful nonsense.

Same with Weight Watchers – no size zero skinny jeans complaining about a millimetre of loose flesh around their waistline. We are all in the same boat. We're all ordinary women – all flawed and all fabulous for it. In a world where we are all supposed to be perfect, it's good to be reminded of that.

AT LARGE
(in a funny old world)

On the Politics of Childcare

When my son moved into first class, although I was sad that he would no longer be in the "babies", it meant he'd be in school until 3pm and I would be getting back a relatively normal working day. As I work from home, I'm one of the lucky ones who can end my working day with my son's.

Clearly the powers that be in Ireland don't want women to work, because if they did they would go the same route as Finland, Sweden and Norway and organise themselves a sensible, workable childcare system, instead of the ridiculous mish-mash that currently exists.

Firstly, the government gives money to a community committee of unqualified lay people (I am on one) to build a childcare facility provided they sacrifice years of their personal, unpaid, unrewarded time to first build and then run it. Ongoing funding for that will be provided on the new subvention scheme. This is a means-tested system that basically means the more children whose parents are receiving benefits, the better funding you will get. If both parents are working, they will have to pay more or less the same as they would if their child was going into one of the many excellent private facilities being squeezed out of the market by ludicrous health-board regulations.

Breege is one of the most qualified and respected early-educators in the country and, in 2008, decided to expand her busy crèche in Ballina town centre to a purpose-built facility on its outskirts. My son did a summer camp there before it opened so I got to take a look around. It is an extremely impressive operation, taking children from birth to after-school. Breege incorporated all of her best ideas and indulged her passion for early year's development with a glass-walled sand room, a dedicated gym and dance room for performances, a state-of-the-art kitchen and lots of cosy chill-out lounge areas. It's child paradise.

But because her build budget was over €800,000, the government gave her no funding. The facility cost her €2 million to build and she had to cover the whole thing herself. On top of that, private places are not entitled to claim subvention. Breege would love to take disadvantaged children on, but there is no funding for her to do that. What this means is immediate class polarisation where poor children will go to state nurseries and posh ones to privates. Et voila – Celtic Tiger class structure at work.

Of course, it can be argued that private crèches are simply running a business – but the reality is they are also running a public service providing working mothers with a safe and nurturing place to leave their children so we can keep our economy going. All the madder, then, that they are being squeezed out of business by health-board regulations which require they provide a luxurious number of toddler toilets when most state schools continue to run with crumbling walls and ancient wash-rooms. While the government gives funding to community crèches, the new system requires them to operate as viable business concerns run by (mostly women) volunteers who, frankly, would much rather spend their evenings sitting in front of the telly with their own children after a hard day's work than filling out ream after ream of government forms.

Of course, none of this would be happening if only women would stay at home and mind the children and stop all of this working nonsense. If they carry on making it this hard, we might just do that.

On Privacy for your Privates

In the hair salon, where Shona provides me with my weekly dose of *Heat* and *Star* magazines, I once saw a picture of Jade Jagger, squatting to have a pee, at a rock festival. Close up. No holds barred. Bare bottomed. That is surely your worst nightmare. We've all been there. The only thing that entered my mind was that old cliché: What is the world coming to?

All females have at one point been caught short, going behind the car, or out on the bog on a walk when husband/sister/offspring shouts "Car coming!" Of course, there isn't a car coming, but by that time it is too late. You have peed on your shoes and they are doubled up with laughter because, of course, catching a lady squatting for a wee is the funniest thing in the whole wide world- unless you are the woman who is weeing.

I do not think that I have ever seen anything more terrible having been done to another human being at the hands of the press in my life. Not the pictures of Britney being carried out of her home strapped to a stretcher or the transcript of Prince Charles' intensely personal ramblings to his then girlfriend Camilla Parker Bowles.

In printing a full page photograph of a woman – any woman – even a jumped up celebrity who was allegedly "in clear view" (of a photographer with a long lens hiding in a van two blocks away) peeing – a line was crossed. It's the line between what should be left to the realms of the imagination and what shouldn't.

If we thought that somebody was too much of a big-shot for us to mix with we were always told to imagine them on the toilet. Most children are told variations of "Even the Queen of England has to go to the toilet," as a reminder that we are all "only human". The only person who didn't have to go to the toilet, I was told, was God. And, of course, the Pope.

My son had a wonderful book called *The Queen's Knickers* in which the Queen, by virtue of adorable line illustrations, is depicted wearing a variety of comely and frilly undergarments according to the occasion she is attending. We got a laugh out of it, and it is delightfully disrespectful whilst at the same time charming and frivolous.

What would not be charming or frivolous is seeing real images of the actual 80-something year old queen in her actual

M & S undies adorning the pages of *Heat* magazine. That would be vile, and more importantly, missing the point. Because the point is that when the lines of what desperate images we can conjure up in our imaginations, and images of actual live events happening, become blurred, the world becomes a scary place.

Surely photography, as a form of visual communication, should be used to at best inform, educate and challenge, and at worst gently titillate – nobody minds a chirpy topless model wibbling her nipples at the nation once she's getting paid a few bob and looks like she doesn't mind too much. Those soft-porn images seem innocent now compared to close up pictures of celebrity cellulite and damp armpits and, as featured in the same issue as Ms. Jagger's bottom – a long lens shot of a celebrity ear revealing that he had – gasp – ear wax!

When will these paps take up residency inside actual toilets? It's certainly where they belong.

On the Merits of Gossip

One of the things that I dislike about celebrity culture is the way it has eroded the old-fashioned tradition of gossip. We no longer need to know what our neighbours are up to because we are too busy watching Jade, Jordan, the Royals, Cruises and Beckhams.

I love gossip and because I am a novelist I am allowed to like it, since I can pretend that sitting around my kitchen table gathering information about the lives of my friends and neighbours is a work resource.

John McGahern was famous for it and most of the writers I know love nothing more than a good old root around the motivations and minutiae of other people's lives.

My mother always taught me there was only one thing worse than being talked about and that was not being talked about. If people said mean things it was because they were jealous. And if people were jealous of you it meant you had "made it".

It was a useful remit to live and work by and generally I don't mind what people say about me behind my back as long as they are nice to my face. In fact, I rather like picking up stuff about myself. Apparently I am a multi-millionaire and once had an affair with my boss- so much more fun than the real thing which is not being a millionaire, multi or otherwise, and not having affairs with anyone at all.

Gossip only really hurts those who care and, of course, some people are more interesting to gossip about than others. The best are the people with 'privacy issues'. Those who wheel themselves out for Mass looking all smart and special, smiling politely - then nobody sees neither hide nor hair of them for the rest of the week.

They don't like people calling to their house, they don't join committees or are ever seen out looking frazzled or moaning about the weather. The women are often elegant and the men friendly but distant. They never go to the local pub, and they do their supermarket shopping outside the local town so nobody knows what they eat. They have a horror of people knowing their business, but what they never realise is aloofness breeds curiosity.

Privacy obsessives like that drive me half mad.

What are they doing in there? I could sit and speculate for hours - and on occasion do. "We're too posh to let people know what we're doing. The plebs couldn't handle it if they knew what we ate for dinner, it's nobody's business but our own." Amateur detectives like me sit around thinking, "Why don't they shop locally? What are they eating in there? Their children? Our missing pets?"

That brand of aloofness is often taken as snobbery, but I don't think that's what it's really about - or even decorum. I think it's about fear. It's about keeping themselves safe from the outside world, not engaging too much with people who are outside of their remit of experience and understanding, and staying in complete control of their environment and of how other people perceive them. I think that must be a very restricting and lonely way to live.

But then what do I know, because bad and all as the ghastly *Celebrity Big Brother* contestants are - they are the opposite of that. Putting every inch of their personalities and bodily functions on show 24/7 for the entertainment of millions. Somehow it's still not as entertaining as speculating about the neighbours. Maybe we should keep our blinds closed and preserve some of life's mystery after all.

On Being a Bit Alternative

In February of 2007, a friend persuaded me to do a detox diet she had found in a health magazine. I did not drop a dress size, but I did get a chronic caffeine withdrawal headache and bad wind. Oh - and a minor spiritual awakening. To distract me from my hunger on Sunday morning the same friend took me for a spin down to Rossport where she was delivering some supplies to the Shell to Sea campaigners campsite.

We drove past Ballycastle, Ceide Fields, Belderrig Harbour and into the heart of that mountainous, sea-edged bogland that for this plastic paddy is the very soul of Ireland. The sun was doing that 'moving spotlight' thing it does across the vast landscapes down here - lighting up sections of a mountain then sweeping across to light up another one.

The Bangor Erris region has always been so astonishingly unspoiled that it's considered more of a national park than a region. The campsite is a nice, friendly set-up, and includes a cosy wooden cabin housing the office and a couple of battered sofas to hang out on, a few substantial-looking tents, a windmill, makeshift toilets - all very eco and quite jolly. We were offered tea and I could have happily settled in there for the night. The protestors were charming and committed. There were some dreadlocked heads, a little ethnic knitwear and, just as I was thinking how interesting it was to be here doing something 'alternative' on a Sunday instead of sitting in some busy pub having a lukewarm roast, I suddenly thought – actually, these people and how they live makes a lot of sense.

It's not a 'lifestyle' in the sense that we know it: replacing working fridges with a Smeg so our friends will think we're cool and then considering ourselves environmentally friendly for not dumping it in our neighbour's skip. These people live their lives, the whole of their lives, with integrity.

I realised that it's me - and the vast majority like me - that are living an 'alternative' life. I believe in all of the things the eco-warriors believe in. I know that multinationals rarely act out of altruistic motives and that politicians often unwittingly and misguidedly act as their puppets. I think we should protect the planet. I say I believe those things but it's just - frankly - too much like hard work to do anything about them. So I live 'alternative' to my belief system - recycling my household waste and throwing a few quid in the direction of relevant causes and pretending to myself that it's enough.

The truth is that I am simply not brave enough to face the truth. Because if I stop long enough and look hard enough at what is happening to the planet, to our landscapes, to our communities, I can't take it in. It's too horrible. So I contain my actions inside the realms of my control; I detox my body so that I don't have to detox the planet.

On our way back we drove past the Shell entrance where all the protests have been going on. The road was lined with traffic cones and there were two buses full of Garda. There was an officious, troubled atmosphere - so completely imported, unlike anything I had ever experienced in this area before. I felt angry, but how angry? Angry enough to go and spend February sleeping in a tent and using an eco loo? Or angry enough to break my diet and tuck into a Kit Kat?

Neither, as it happens. Tomorrow I'll wake up toxin-free. But what good will it do me in the long run?

On Good Manners and Decency

One year my friend, a PE teacher in a Mayo girls' school, took four busloads of her kids up to Dublin for a school league basketball final. They are a pretty mixed bunch from backgrounds representative of the national average - all types of homes, middle class, Traveller, a few foreign nationals, some wealthier girls- as one would expect from a largish state school. My friend is a tough cookie. She keeps them in line but has always conceded they are a pretty cool bunch of people. She's proud of them.

They were playing girls from a reputable, expensive, private convent girls' school in south County Dublin - "the cream of the country", as they are popularly described.

When my friend's school team came out onto the court, one of their rival team was heard to say, loudly, "You can smell the poverty off them," and when the girls from the state school began to do their cheerleading routine their rivals, who were already beating them in the game, turned their backs to them and drowned out their rehearsed performance by shouting, "Who Let the Dogs Out."

What my friend found most shocking was not the girls' behaviour (we all know how nasty girls can be), but the fact that their teachers did not reprimand them or stop the cruel chanting. The Mayo girls were genuinely upset. This was a big day out for them, and after an exhausting journey it was horrible for them to be faced with this kind of, what I would call, class abuse. We are urban, we are rich, ergo, we are better than you.

As is often the case, the reality is very different to the perception. This Mayo state school has a very high standard of education - it just does not discriminate in who receives it. However, that is not the point. The point is that these girls felt entitled to trash them because they have been told that they are 'better', if not by their parents then by our bigger-is-better 'new Ireland' society.

It is not the breakdown of the Catholic Church that is gradually turning us into a nation of rude, ignorant hogs. It is the handbag-worshipping, Porsche-driving, aspirant mind-set that is encouraging us to look down on people because they have less money than us. What hope have we got for the future if we are really turning from the land of saints and scholars into a nouveau riche haven?

An English friend of mine, visiting me for the weekend in Dublin, was extremely amused by what she found in Brown Thomas. "All these women ostentatiously shouting over each other about how much they were spending on a handbag. It was hilarious." I was enraged at her amusement and defended our 'new money' ethos… poverty for centuries, 800 years of oppression, etc.

But the reality is, showing off how much money you have is not clever; it always looks tacky and cheap. Sending your children to an expensive school and then encouraging them to think that they are better than other children with less money or education does not make you posh. It makes you ignorant. Good taste cannot be bought and respect is not something you can throw money at. You have to earn it the old fashioned way with good manners and decency.

My friend's team lost, but their supporters cheered them on from beginning to end. Nobody left the field. They also got the prize for best halftime entertainment, despite the cruel taunting. In that sense they were the true winners of the day.

On Giving a Goat for Christmas

"I don't want a goat for Christmas. I want a new handbag or a piece of jewellery." The thing about charity gifts is that nobody believes that anyone will actually want them. In fairness the only reason I really genuinely do want a goat, or a pig, or a house for somebody else on Christmas is because that year I had gone to Guatemala to visit charity projects with Trocaire. I was there so that I could come back and help promote their Global Gift Campaign. You would imagine the whole thing would make me feel as if I was a marvellous human being... but it didn't. It just made me realise how thoroughly useless I am and reprogrammed my guilt genes to include world poverty.

The trip ranks among the most extraordinary, moving experiences of my life. I received hospitality from people who had virtually nothing to give; one family in the wake of hurricane damage had nothing to eat and no clean water. I met an extraordinary midwife who had delivered one hundred children and only recently learned how to sterilise and utilise scissors. She pleaded with me to help train midwives like her so they could save lives.

Her midwife kit had been washed away in the recent storms and I thought, a pair of scissors. One pair of effing scissors... then I came back to Santa lists and requests to bring back cashmere sweaters from French Connection in Luton Duty Free. It was unbearable, really.

What coming face to face with poverty, hardship and injustice did for me personally was turn me from a shallow, selfish greedy bitch who thought I was a generous charity giver into a selfish, greedy bitch who knows that she doesn't give nearly enough to the needy. My scant consolation is that I now understand that the only people in the western world who are not selfish, greedy bitches are people like Christina Noble who devote their entire lives to helping the poor.

Giving is necessary because it makes me feel better about myself. It makes me feel like I'm a good person. But when I recall the midwives, the small farmers, the struggling families with hordes of poverty-stricken children in Guatemala I realise how little I am prepared to do. I imagine that I would like to go over there and devote a couple of years actively to help ... but of course with a young family, and my settled life here, it's impossible.

Actually I'm fooling myself, because I have imagined all sorts of impossible things, including becoming a novelist, moving to the country, finding a week to travel to the Sahara on my own, and managed to make them happen. It's all about commitment. If I relinquished two of my bedrooms and made do with one car the money I would save could make a huge difference to hundreds of lives. It's a reality.

What I can do, however, is continue to face up and keep the memory of what I experienced alive so that I can pass it on. So that when somebody says to me, "I don't want a goat. I want a handbag," I can be as politically correct and self-righteous as I am when somebody says the word 'nigger'.

There are people who are prepared to give their lives to helping others and the very, very least I can do is buy people goats for Christmas, and encourage them to do the same for me. On the plus side I was astonished by the response I got for my Trocaire gifts last year. My father-in-law was gratifyingly thrilled when I presented him with a 'pig'.

On Low Level Hypochondria

Since when did the human condition become a disease? It seems that low level hypochondria is all pervasive in our society. I think it's because our expectations of life are too high. We expect that we should feel happy and full of energy and fun all the time, and when we don't we think there is something wrong.

I have seen too many people go half out of their minds with grief because they had a chest infection, and then take to the bed with depression because of the effects of the antibiotics. I think I would have preferred it in the old days when people gave birth in fields and dropped dead from consumption cutting turf. Getting on with the business of staying alive until . . . BAM . . . time's up.

Imagine a world before you asked people, "How are you?" and they actually told you. The freedom of not having to listen to your whinging friend (we all have one) regaling you with the boring minutia of her daily ups and downs. The days when you didn't have to worry about the shape of your thighs because (a) they were like moulded steel from walking backwards and forwards to the well and (b) nobody, probably not even your husband, ever got to see them.

We are so bloody precious about ourselves these days. Going to homeopaths and spending 20 on two millilitres of bottled water for some imagined ailment. 'Stress' is what most of it seems to come down to. And yet, what really have most of us got to be stressed about? Nothing. Stress is a useless modern invention . . . more painful than the Brazilian wax and more pointless than the hostess trolley.

People who are starving or dying don't get stressed; they get sad. Perhaps we get stressed to stop ourselves feeling guilty about all the real sadness in the world. Because, after all, you might internalise other people's sadness and that can lead to chest infections! Or depression, another bandied about term.

Depression is a misunderstood ailment, and that is partly because it has become so commonly used to describe how one feels when not on top of the world. Many real depressives remain undiagnosed because they are afraid that their very real symptoms are just them being self-indulgent. The reason for this is because so many of us are, now, self-indulgent about our feelings. We can't cope with the stress of work or not having been hugged enough as a child, so we get 'depressed'. Not depressed enough to seek medical care, or kill ourselves (as friends of mine with real depression have done) but depressed enough to call it 'depression' and garner sympathy and comfort from indulgent friends and family.

I just think this kind of emotional and physical hypochondria somehow takes from those people who are truly suffering. Selfish miserable attention-seekers who used to be told to "get on with it" are now able to take centre stage in our sympathetic, permissive society. Where does the line between genuine hardship and indulgent neurosis end?

On Why Celebrity Marriages are a Disaster

Is there a person alive who doesn't know enough about the egocentric nature of celebrity to realize that it is completely contrary to the idea of marriage? Or more to the point, do we really understand what marriage is anymore? Marriage - real, working, stick-it-out marriage - has become, like the realities of childbirth, a dark secret nobody ever tells you about until it's too late. Like meeting The Perfect One, pain-free natural childbirth, and working women who successfully juggle their lives, Happily Ever After is a fantasy we invented. It has backfired and serves only to make our lives more complicated and difficult than they already are.

While our grandparents groaned and got-on-with-it, taking the whole 'in sickness and in health' thing to heart and staying together for lifetimes – what we have now is a culture where marriage is presented as the perfect ending to the perfect love story and the ultimate expression of love. You love somebody *so much* that you feel like you want to spend the rest of your life with them. And so you tie yourselves in with a ten grand day out and a legal contract and sit back to enjoy the endless hot date you have been promised. Like heaven, marriage is love that lasts forever. When the love goes, or you get bored or fed up, you end the marriage. Unless, of course, your husband is a really good looking footballer, in which case you might let them disrespect you with some topless dolly one more time - because you love them. And that's what marriage is all about, isn't it? Being in love?

Except of course, it isn't. Actually, for most normal human beings, (the honest ones because loads of people lie about being madly in love because there is such pressure, even on oneself, to keep the dream of romantic love alive), marriage is the challenge of living with somebody after the love has gone. The sacrifice of oneself for the betterment and happiness of the other person even – especially – when you don't feel like it. Marital love is the grown up stuff that happens when the feeling of love has faded and you have to be nice anyway so that the *actual* love – the results of the hard stuff like dealing with their ghastly relatives, tolerating their annoying little habits, biting your tongue when she gains three stone after the baby, eating the meal he cooked (even though the meat was slightly underdone) so as not to hurt his feelings, the not putting him down in front of the kids, or laughing cruelly at her attempts to look fashionable after forty – has the chance to grow and settle.

Marriage is hard work, and it takes time and commitment. Seemingly, being a celebrity is bloody hard work too. I mean, more work than the rest of us can ever know in that weird, unsettling way that young people now seem to aspire to. Two hours in hair and make-up for Cheryl, hours of training for Ashley – just enough recreation time to be photographed coming out of Nobu, or throwing a few shapes around Chinawhite, or a five minute sofa-lounge with a lap dancer in Stringfellows. What about scrounging a couple of hours on a Saturday to watch the match at the pub, or trying to escape off with your girlfriends shopping for an afternoon because you've spent all week gawking at the telly in parallel partner mode and you're sick of the sight of each other. Celebrities don't have the luxury, or irritation, of living on top of one another because they are too busy being celebrities.

Ashley Cole is idolized and paid an enormous amount of money for playing football. Cheryl has lovely hair and can sing and dance, and for this she has to spend a third of her working day getting all dolled up, and is held up as a role model for millions of young girls.

Our young men want to be rich footballers and our young women want to be married to them, forever and ever – one long hot date for the rest of our lives. Does anyone else see the flaw in this picture?

What are we are telling kids about marriage and how to choose their life partners? Wait until you fall hopelessly, madly in love, then get married and live happily ever after. Marriage is, after all, the reward for meeting Mr. Right. Once you've met a man who you are stone mad crazy about, then everything will fall into place. Surely, with all these famous Alpha men sowing their seed left, right and centre, causing pain and chaos and leaving their loyal, long-suffering wives reeling and gritting their teeth, we should be guiding our daughters towards settling for a nice ordinary lad with a decent job, even if he is a bit dull.

But no. What we want, what we *all* want, is the man with an ego and a following the size of Wembley Stadium who, by some freakish turn of nature, will be satisfied with a kiss and a cuddle and a pizza in front of Emmerdale with the same woman for the rest of his life. Not going to happen. Is there any evidence, anywhere, that this man exists?

There is also the element of wanting what we want when we want it- instant gratification. Cheryl seems like a lovely girl who, coming from a difficult background, doubtless craved the security of marriage. Society let her down by selling her the fib that marriage equals security and safety.

Marriage offers more security to the faithless liar than the innocent trier. She is torn because a bit of paper - quickly and fecklessly legalized - means that, despite having been humiliated by a spoiled teenage boy, she can't just walk away. She has to follow due procedure. He gets to beg her to stay, and get the public to row in and persuade her to give him "one more chance".

Of course, it's nonsense. Men don't muck about at that level by unhappy accident. Mucky men are mucky men. They don't make good husbands. Ever. End of story.

While entertainers are generally weird, flawed, egocentric, often insecure people, the effect of celebrity on a young, impressionable male has to be ruinous.

When Ashley was caught out the first time, Cheryl's mother-in-law moved in to their house. Part of his defence now is that the MIL moving in put a dampener on his and Cheryl's thrilling sex life. Sorry son, if at your age and stage of fitness you can't get it on in an enormous mock-tudor hacienda with your mother-in-law under the same roof – your problems are only just beginning. By the same token, Cheryl, did you honestly think a football hero was going to tolerate you pursuing a career as an international pop star? Did nobody tell you the deal? When you marry a Premiership footballer, you put your life on hold and dedicate yourself entirely to him in the hope that he might possibly remain loyal and faithful to you – or at least, not disrespect you too publicly.

And yet, at heart, our public interest in train wreck celebrity marriages surely just reflects our own broken hopes and dreams. We still want the fairy-tale. We want to believe in loyalty, and respect, and trust and true love lasting forever and marriage being one hot steamy date. But wanting something, as Cheryl and Ashley Cole have discovered recently, isn't always enough.

KATE KERRIGAN

On the Grotesqueness of the Celtic Tiger Years

The Shelbourne Hotel had launched their summer drinks list. At the top of the menu they invited us to "Drink Pink" – with a glass of Pink Champagne de Castellane at €18, or while not try "The New Cosmo" a confection called Glamour Gal for a mere €11.50? I wondered how many of those it would take to convince the ageing tigress, with her too-tanned bingo wings and sun-crepe-cleavage as she tipples at the bar in a Versace leopard-print slip, that the separated bloated banker eyeing her up looks like George Clooney.

Doubtless there are a few people who can afford to be genuinely discerning enough to prefer a Pink Prosecco Valdo to say – an ordinary one. I don't know them – thank God – but doubtless there is still a smattering of moneyed fusspots around. However, one wonders if there is anyone left stupid enough to be still pulled in by the whole 'lifestyle' marketing angle. Is there anyone, really, left who has so little else to do with their time and money that they might be persuaded that an evening "Drinking Pink" is not only pointlessly spendthrift but dare I say it – rather naff?

Some of us sat out the excesses of Celtic Tiger, myself among them. I didn't spend a thousand euro on a handbag or splash out on any Manolos. Any spare cash we had went into a few nice paintings and knocking our kitchen wall down and putting a new roof on the extension. We did some nice things during the good times – footed the bill on a couple of big family celebrations, had a few holidays, bought a second hand Mercedes - but I always found the conspicuous consumption unattractive. I never aspired to dressing like a British footballer's wife, or winning Best Dressed in Galway (although I judged it once in my fashion magazine days – and gave it to a cheaply dressed young fashion student for which I was berated horribly). Perhaps it is the middle-class Mayo stock I come from, but flashy cars and designer gear have never done it for me. "That's just showing off," my grandmother used to say – although I can't remember what she was saying it about now. Any notion of what "showing off" in Ireland used to be – a new coat, a car, a gaudy garden gnome, a colour television set – has surely been buried with the ten bedroom balconied haciendas, Ferraris and five-grand handbags of the past ten years.

The recession, I thought (hoped) would curb the nations excesses, not just from a fiscal point of view, but also from a style one. Put bluntly, it is now unfashionable to "show off". Any style icon worth their salt is "Mixing and matching" their three-season-old designer gear with high street. Not because they have to, but because rubbing other people's noses in how much money you have is now considered crude and distasteful. Yet the success of the *Sex and The City* movie suggests that we are still craving the ludicrous lifestyle of Cosmos and sitting about in cocktail bars in killer heels talking about – well – *what* actually? To my mind if your girlfriends are so boring that you need to spend two hours in rollers, covering yourself in lip-gloss and glitter before traipsing miles in a taxi to sit up at a mirrored bar getting hammered on €15 (pink!) cocktails in order to enjoy their company, frankly there must be something missing. If you enjoy the company of your friends, surely a bag of Tayto and a pint will do the trick just as well. You might want to throw on a clean blouse, or cover up the late-night baby-bags under your eyes with a bit of foundation – but surely all this artifice and effort is no longer necessary.

Did we learn nothing in those ten years? We all know why we ran away with ourselves. Centuries of poverty and repression meant we all felt we had something to prove. Well, now we've proved it. We can be just as tasteless and vacuous and easily led by the glitter of glamour and the promise of wealth as the "Loads-a-money" Thatcher generation of 80's Britain. Surely now it is time to turn our backs on the excesses. There is no need to hang our heads in shame or go back to the bad old days of negative poor-mouthing – but at least let's foster an atmosphere of dignity and decorum, where intelligence and wit and social morality are valued above the fluff of fashion. It's not going to be easy because we have got used to the flash and the finery. Denied it for so long, we grabbed on tight to the trappings of wealth – but now it's time to let them go.

What we can learn from this time is to distinguish what is important and what is stupid indulgence. We don't need to drink alcohol that is specifically pink- not any more. We are over that. We also don't need to go on regular Spa Weekend breaks, or spend fifteen-hundred euro on a handbag, or to queue for five hours to buy "eco-friendly" shopping bags by Anya Hindemarch (guilty!), or have weekly manicures, or drive yellow sports cars or go on shopping trips to New York every Christmas, or have an all-year-round tan. We do not need a Burberry baby blanket or a diamante collar for our dog. There is no need for any of that because we do not live in Manhattan or Hollywood, and we are not ghastly British Chavs. We live in Ireland - which means we go to the pub and have the craic and don't notice or care if our friend's bag was bought in Brown Thomas or Penneys – we like it anyway. Let's be the unpretentious Irish again. After all - that's what's we're famous for the world over.

KATE KERRIGAN

On Forbidden Topics of Conversation

I once had a heated argument with somebody that nearly resulted in a horrible falling-out. Over nutrition. I was arguing that "Doctor" Gillian McKeith was a charlatan and that it was a disgrace that wannabe health professionals, who can't be bothered to go to university and study for ten years to be real doctors, go around masquerading as experts and con people into paying them money for treatments and pseudo-medical professional advice which they are, frankly, not qualified to give. My friend was arguing that we all eat a load of crap and that at least McKeith gives an obese, food-ignorant society sound nutritional advice, regardless of whether she's a real doctor or not.

"Who cares," she argued, "as long as what she says is sensible and helps people stay alive?"

"I care!" I shouted, "Because I am fed up with idiots telling me mung beans can stop me dying of cancer!"

"Maybe they can!" she shouted.

"That's, that's, that's... scientifically unproven!" I yelled.

"No, it isn't," she yelled back. "They are full of vitamins and are very good for you!"

In fairness, this person is at least 20 years older than me, two stone lighter, and springs out of bed each morning at six in the morning full of energy, then powers through the day with admirable gusto fuelled by an impeccable vegetarian diet rich in proteins, complex carbohydrates and, doubtless, mung beans.

I, on the other hand, have to haul my objecting, sugar-infected body down to a cupboard full of supplements, washed down with two strong cups of coffee, before I can persuade it to function at all.

What was interesting to me was less the details of what we were disagreeing about, but the fact that we became so exercised about it. This has happened to me a lot of late. I have found myself pontificating on the subject of why alternative remedies are scientifically unsound, or why I elected to have a Caesarean section, or joking that my child eats nothing that hasn't been processed into the shape of a cartoon character first – and really seeming to offend people. As if the details of how we look after ourselves as individuals has become the ethics of how we live collectively.

Politics and religion used to be no-go impolite topics of conversation. Now, one wouldn't dream of questioning somebody's religious beliefs. It would be rudeness bordering on xenophobia to question somebody's personal relationship with God (or not God, as the case may be). Ditto politics. You might argue a point on principle, but don't undermine a person's loyalty to a party. Don't go there.

The area where I do go, and where I am beginning to question whether I should, is in the ethics of personal behaviour. Botox or not? Alternative remedies: do they work? Should we be eating GM foods? Are elective Caesareans "wrong"? Will mung beans protect you from cancer?

We don't care about the dos and don'ts of philosophical, human questions like "an eye for an eye" versus "turn the other cheek", or the social interests of the disadvantaged against the necessities of world economy. The ethics we're slugging out now are: is it prudent to inject one's face with rat poison in order to freeze one's wrinkles, will homeopathy work on your corns, and should you be eating McDonalds or mung beans? Seems like we've become so shallow that we've nothing proper left to argue about…

On Being Fat

Nigella finally sold out and lost weight. I hate that. With her posh drawling voice and her finger-licking and her "yummy" low-cut tops and her luscious hair dipping into the fondant icing, let's face it- the only thing she had going for her as a cheering role model for the harassed housewife was the fact that she was a bit plump.

Not Dawn French proper plump mind, that might warm your heart, but a kind of sexy, eats-the-occasional-Mars Bar-and-just-gets-away-with-it plump, which is something for your average lumpy broad to aspire to. Now there she was on the cover of a food magazine this week looking "forget it" thin. Skinny white arms struggling to hold up a tray of buns, huge teeth and looking suspiciously younger and wrinkle free. It really annoyed me.

You don't have to look like a fashion model to be a good cook, but it helps. You also don't have to look like a fashion model to be a good actress or a good novelist, but it seems it helps with those things also. The only people to whom it makes a difference to look like a fashion model to are, newsflash, fashion models!

So why, why, *why* are we doing this to ourselves, ladies?

Do men want us to be skinny, white-toothed, Botox-faced Stepford wives? No. Is it attractive, really, this homogenised, size-zero grinning skeletal look? No. Do we really want to be known throughout history as the generation who made the handbag-wider-than-your-waist look fashionable? Actually, I no longer think that this skinniness obsession is a fashion thing. I think there is something inherently wrong with us women. Fat is not a feminist issue insofar as I don't think it has anything to do with men any more. Fat is a female issue.

I am cross with Nigella because now I feel I have to lose a stone. Not that I haven't felt I had to lose at least a stone for the whole of my adult life, including when I was weighing in at a light-as-a-fart seven and a half stone. Gradually with age common sense has begun to kick in, insofar as I can feel the tides turning where my ambition is no longer to be stick thin, but rather to be whatever size my appetite for food decrees and not care what that size is. But it's not that easy.

I had to stop myself from watching another documentary about the size double-zero debacle this week because part of my dysfunctional mind would be thinking, "Hmm… 12 litres of water a day and one protein bar a fortnight . . . I could do that." It seems that, despite the media attempts to convince us that extreme dieting is dangerous and stupid, we cannot get it out of our heads that life would be much easier and better if we were thin. But would it really?

I'm five-foot-nothing and once got so skinny I had to shop in the children's department of Dunne's. It was during a brief period of my life where I was deeply unhappy and smoked sixty fags a day.

Was it worth it? No, not really. Except it meant I got to wear a bikini and enjoy it for the first time in my adult life.

On balance, though, I'd trade the bikini for enough flesh on my hips to hold up a pair of size 12 (okay, 10!) jeans, a fag-free lifestyle and a thriving relationship with my biscuit tin.

I just wish I didn't have to spend so much time reassuring myself that I'm okay as I am.

On My Extraordinary Experience of Women in Africa

I was sitting across a standard conference-room desk listening to the story of Florence Anyango. She was a softly spoken Kenyan woman in her 40s, I would say, although I surmise that more from the breadth of her extraordinary and terrible life experience than her appearance. Florence's husband beat her and her children for the entire length of their 24-year marriage. She endured humiliation and abuse few of us can imagine before managing to escape him with the help of the Coalition on Violence Against Women (CoVAW), an organisation part-funded by Trócaire, at whose invitation I was visiting various women-focused projects in Kenya.

We met in a charming colonial building on the outskirts of Nairobi where CoVAW's offices were situated. The lush, green suburbs of this city belied the constant threat of violent crime in this, one of the most dangerous places in the world. Kenya has a shocking gap between rich and poor, with the 'haves' living in relative luxury, albeit with 24-hour security and 12ft electric fences, and the 'have-nots' living in dire poverty - one in five Nairobians is estimated to live in Kibera, the biggest slum in Africa, where the conditions beggar belief.

Interviewing Florence, however, it was clear that money and class did not protect women against violence. Neither - until very recently in Kenya - did the law. Forty-nine per cent of women in this popular safari holiday destination are said to have experienced physical violence, and that's before you consider other basic human-rights abuses. Women constitute 54% of Kenya's voting population but occupy only 4% of its parliamentary seats. 80% of Kenyan agricultural workers are women, yet they own just 5% of the land.

International Women's Day is on 8 March. That's when women celebrate their emancipation in various ways throughout the world. But in some places there won't be any celebration. In some regions of Kenya, adult women can be forced to marry without their consent. Through a practice called cleansing, a widow can be 'inherited' by a close relative of her deceased husband or she can be forced to have sex with a social outcast to remove the spirits of her deceased husband. An estimated 38% of Kenyan women between 15 and 49 years old had undergone female genital mutilation (FGM) before the practice was made illegal in 2001 - although, according to the women's groups we spoke to, the ban has had little bearing on this brutal ancient tradition, merely sending the practice underground and making it harder to monitor.

Like many African countries, Kenya has been ravaged by the HIV/AIDS epidemic and women appear to be the most affected. Men believe that women carry the virus, and once a woman is infected the man will abandon her and move on to infect another woman - leaving her to fend for herself and any children. Another dangerous myth circulating is that sex with a virgin can cure AIDS. This has precipitated a terrible rise in young girls - and very small children - presenting as victims of rape.

Until very recently, marital rape was not recognised as a crime here. According to UN estimates, 42% of Kenyan women are battered by their husbands or partners. Women back home are beaten too, of course, and as I sit there listening to Florence's story I find myself getting emotional. Not in the usual social-conscience way that I am familiar with, having done these types of trips before, but because I could identify with her story.

I have experienced domestic violence in my family. It was a long time ago, but suddenly, without warning, in another continent, in this professional setting, all my old hurt and anger - embarrassingly messy emotions - rose up in me and made me, inappropriately and annoyingly, start to cry. And I realised that, despite my understanding of social conscience, this was my first true point of contact with it. Because it is only when social conscience becomes personal conscience that things really start to happen. For instance, I think it's terrible that so many women in the developing world are being denied their basic human rights. Darfur? Shocking! But frankly, I'm just so snowed under with my own human rights right now - I just don't know where to start. I've got a job, investments, I'm juggling homework, housework, a second mortgage, I've got a husband to boss about and, on top of it all, can anyone tell me what's going on in fashion right now? There is nothing - *nothing* - for the big-busted woman in need of tailoring this season.

Like most pampered women in the western world I think having glossy, well-cut hair is a human right and consider my inability to live up to the consumer mantra 'Because I'm worth it' with monthly facials a kind of martyrdom. I can afford to be blasé about my life because my grandmother and my mother fought centuries of injustice and prejudice to earn my generation the right to be frivolous. We have shown our gratitude by embracing the breast-enhancement/Botox culture whilst complaining loudly that men today are 'too nice'.

That is why Africa was such a shock to me.

Because when poverty - spiritual, emotional, physical poverty - comes close enough that you can touch it by hand it stops being about social conscience, and becomes personal. Personal enough that you want to do something about it - that you want to make the pain go away. Which is why the generations of women before us bothered chaining themselves to railings and stood up to the bullying tyrants of a patriarchal society. Because their lives were crap and they didn't want ours to be the same.

And that is what a handful of women - and men - in Kenya are doing, too.

Trying hard to smile, Agnes Leina is one of them. An astonishingly beautiful Masai woman, with sculptured cheekbones and a ready smile, she is full of enthusiasm and laughter - despite the nature of her work as programme officer for CoVAW. Close to her heart is the problem of FGM and forced marriage among Masai girls. She was excited to meet someone from Ireland, as she studied here in Kimmage in Dublin. She was interested in hearing about our Travelling community because the Masai are pastoralists and she can identify with them. She was horrified when I told her what - pathetically little - I knew about their struggle to get halting sites in Ireland, and the racism and prejudice they face. Whatever the Kenyan government is doing to the pastoralists with regard to selling off land, they are not trying to get them to 'settle'.

Agnes took us to a school for girls who have escaped and been rescued from FGM. We crowded into the headmistress' office and underwent the formal introductions that seem to be a tradition here. All meetings begin with each person explaining themselves - like group therapy: "My name's Kate and I'm a writer," I said a dozen times a day - smiling. I kept on smiling - I smiled at everyone all the time. Partly because I didn't know what to say and partly because all I was thinking was, how do you stomach this suffering? Girls being cut to shreds then married off at eight years old. "If they are lucky he will already have a wife who might look after her."

Agnes mimed a gesture of a child being held down. "It is the women who are the custodians of these traditions," somebody else said. It was gruelling listening and one meeting in which I gave up smiling.

Afterwards we walked around the school and I couldn't meet the children's eyes. I kept thinking about my nine-year-old niece. From there we went to a tiny craft shop owned by Peninah Tombo in Kajiado. She had undergone FGM as a young girl but was rescued from a planned forced early marriage and was able to stay in school. She eventually married a middleclass Kenyan man (that's a man with a job) and began selling jewellery made by her old Masai friends, Elizabeth, Jemima and Grace, to raise money to send girls to school. Very few tribal girls are encouraged towards education - once they are circumcised and married, their schooling stops. Their shop is far from the safari tourist trail and I wonder how they make money at all. Actually, they struggle and are thrilled to see us. We, in turn, are thrilled to shop and spend money. For one hour it is bangles and baubles and smiles all around, but as we drive away I am plunged into depression wondering how they maintain hope with such small gestures weighed against such massive problems.

Trócaire highlighted some of these problems that year in its evocative and challenging advertising campaign. The TV ad showed a number of babies who all have one thing in common that could put them at risk of experiencing those problems - the fact that they are girls. The Trócaire box showed baby Amina from Malawi, whose mother's wish as she sang her to sleep was that her future would be better than hers, that she will have the chance to go to school and won't have to work in the fields to survive.

Despair on behalf of other people's problems, though, is unseemly. I see it in the eyes of every Trócaire staff member but none of them would ever be tacky enough to say it. "I couldn't handle the poverty," is the reason so many people give for not visiting the developing world on holidays - for going straight from airport coach to hotel compound. The implication is that they have an abounding amount of sensitivity. In actual fact, it is not sensitivity but guilt that prevents us from looking.

Those who can look - NGO workers, missionary workers - do so. They certainly have as much sensitivity but perhaps they have less guilt.

The next day we learned that things were not all bleak in Kenya. Until very recently the law had not recognised domestic violence as a specific crime. However, in 2006 a new Sex Act was passed which not only recognises rape as a problem, but specifies a minimum sentence of ten years for rape and life imprisonment for "defilement of a child". It's a wide-reaching law which has the potential to transform the lives of Kenyan women, but it has been a long time coming and is in no small part due to the tireless campaigning of organisations like CoVAW and LVCT (Liverpool Voluntary Testing and Counselling), a HIV/AIDS NGO that has pioneered rape-crisis centres in Kenyan hospitals.

Hadley (mercifully a man!) showed us around the rape unit at Kenyatta General Hospital in Nairobi. The systems they had set up were impressive. A woman or child presented within 48 hours of being raped will be tested for HIV and given PEP (post-exposure prophylaxis) to reduce the chance of becoming HIV infected. The woman or child will then be given a medical exam to gather necessary legal evidence. There is counselling on hand, as well as a police and legal presence - so it is in effect a one-stop shop for rape victims.

That's the good news. The bad news is that there are a huge amount of them and Kenyatta Hospital is pitifully short of resources. The psychiatrist who runs the unit, Dr Ian Kanyanya, is working in the oldest part of the hospital without as much as a computer or a proper screen for educational presentations. They are short of chairs in the group counselling room. The spirit is there, the law is behind them - but the resources are falling very, very short. "We have been open since last September but we are afraid to advertise the fact that we are here because we will not be able to handle the influx, "he said.

On our last day we visit the slums of Nakuru where a diminutive Northern Irish nun, Sr. Patricia Speight, runs the Love and Hope Foundation, offering counselling and home nursing assistance to people with AIDS. It is not gender specific work - but she assures us that women always come off worse here. The conditions are dire. Open sewers, children dying, prostitution.

The people we met on the programme were charming, intelligent and, above all, grateful, willing themselves to live and, in part, with Sr. Patricia's help, succeeding. We met women and men alike here - poverty and death are surely the great equalisers.

I came home tired, weepy and with a lot of gratitude of my own. Learning something of the lives of the Kenyans made me more aware that we still have our own battles to fight, our own abused and needy women to champion and protect. But it also made me realise that if I am a global citizen - enjoying the benefits of world travel, buying coffee grown in Kenya, runners made in Vietnam, handbags produced in China - then I hold communal responsibility for their welfare above and beyond my ability to holiday and shop.

But then, that's just theory. Being a sensitive person with a social conscience never saved lives - unless you are willing to do something about it.

On An Extraordinary Man

One of the things that I am most proud of about being Irish is the Irish wake. Of course, there are those who think of it as an "imposition" and request the silent privacy preferred by the English – but I think that's a shame. There is something 'right' about facing death. What could be more honest than displaying a familiar face so that everyone who loved and respected them gets the chance to say goodbye? Less maudlin than fully honoring a person's life by socialising around them in a vigil? More supportive than neighbours taking over your kitchen – filling it with food and company and generosity? Proximity to death, both our own and other people's teaches us the most important lessons about life. Very recently my good friend Sinead lost her father. And he was, a very great loss, not just to his family, but the community of North West Mayo. At his funeral mass it was standing room only right through the car park. There were eighteen priests on the tiny alter – his wife Frankie and six children filled a full pew – and I thought – he must have been an extraordinary man. From the few times I met him I could tell he was an imppecably mannered old school gentleman - like my grandfather. A devout, respectable, pioneer who used his intelligence to do good things for people. A decent man. And so I grieved, not just for Paul Leonard and his family, but for the quality of generosity, decency, the uncompromising practice of Christian values that marked out extraordinary men of that generation. Today we aspire to mark ourselves out as extraordinary by being thinner, richer, having better cars, bigger houses than our neighbours. "Goodness" is not an achievement. "Decency" is not acknowledged as a quality. Last year Vincent, my grandmother's next door neighbour died, but not before he had cut enough turf to see his widow through the following winter. Her cousin John, when he knew he wasn't going to see Christmas, bought and sent all of his Christmas cards in November. Mindful of others – in the small ways that matter, right to the end.

Are there still compassionate auctioneer's like my friend's father who can be trusted to look after the affairs of the elderly and the needy? Men with humility who are never boastful, or flashy although they might have both reason and means to be both? And while I was sitting in Killala church listening to Paul's eulogy I thought – is this the last generation of this kind of 'ordinary' yet extraordinary men? What will they be saying about my generation of high achievers; "He had wall mounted flat-screen TV in every room and a Lamborghini by the time he was fifty. He upgraded his house and his wives six times in a lifetime?"

It is depressing to think that the very qualities that mark us as outstanding human beings; self-sacrifice, kindness, generosity of spirit – have become so unfashionable. So dwarfed by modern passions of glamour and instant gratification.

I looked then at the front pew which was filled with Paul's children and I realised that they all have at least one thing in common; a social conscience. They are all, in one way or another, involved or interested in some kind of social or community activism.

Paul Leonard's legacy of decency is in his children, how they live their lives and what they pass on of that to their children.

So even in these selfish times, it's still possible for parents to hand on a strong moral legacy, if we are willing to mark ourselves out from the pack.

With what he has left behind him, Paul Leonard will surely Rest In Peace.

On Art

I have always loved art. Like almost every child up to the age of ten, my Picasso-fan parents considered me something of an abstract finger-painting art prodigy – until my teens when my very modest talents gave way to hanging around art galleries wearing bohemian '80s blouses and lots of black eyeliner hoping to pick up an older art student boyfriend.

None of this led to a place at art school as I hoped it might and so I had to content myself with being an art consumer. For a long time this meant simply going to galleries. As a journalist, I hung about on the edges of the art world and went to countless exhibition openings looking at wonderful stuff produced by young Irish artists, drinking in work by the likes of David Godbold thinking, "Gosh that's fantastic." But never, for one moment, did I think of actually buying anything. For some reason, buying art just did not seem feasible. Occasionally I would go to a posh house and see wonderful paintings hanging, but I always just assumed that original, contemporary art was something that materialised miraculously in the homes of people with taste and money, like heirloom antiques and couture. Covetable, sure, but not for me.

Then something happened which changed everything. One of my friends opened a gallery.

When the Paul Kane Gallery opened in 1997 we all trooped up the stairs of his South William Street space on opening night. I thought I was in seventh heaven. A white-walled haven, just around the corner from my apartment, and I could pop in there any time I wanted and take in real 'art'.

One day I called in and stood for ages looking at a copper and red heathery landscape by Margaret Deignan.

"I love that," I said.

"Why don't you buy it?" said Paul.

I blushed, and if it had been any other gallery in the world I would have run out and never gone back. But because it was Paul I said, "How much is it?"

"£185," he said. Then looking at my shell-shocked expression he added, "You can pay me in instalments."

I bought it and hung it up in my apartment and felt very grown-up and pleased with myself. I still have the landscape and enjoy it every day. It has – I discovered only in writing this article – quadrupled in value in 10 years. Which is a lot more than can be said for my prize bonds, bank savings or properties.

In the past decade my husband and I have bought a lot of art. Not enough to fill a warehouse or a holiday villa in Cannes and we don't own a Louis Le Brocquy or a Damian Hirst. We're not rich. It's just that we have come to value art more than designer duds or golfing holidays in the Algarve.

So that when I visit a lavishly decorated interior space, be it a hotel or private house, and there is something nasty and makey-up on the walls, I notice it – and it makes me mad. Why is it that when every county in Ireland is bursting at the seams with talented artists who could transform an interior space for the price of a three-seater sofa – that so many decorators choose instead to spend the money on elaborate light fittings and either skimp on the art, or encourage the owner to put up representative landscapes by his wife's friend, for which he will have paid a small fortune?

Bad art in hotels is a particular bugbear. The interior designers go to trouble and expense to procure plush furnishings and stain-friendly carpets, then go and buy a job lot of ghastly prints to put on the walls. Or worse, the TV designers' version: "Get three blank canvasses and paint them different shades of blue, then hang them next to each other."

A notable exception to this is the Ice House in Ballina. It had been sold to me as having great food, state-of-the-art spa – so far so every other new hotel, but the first thing I noticed when I walked through this extraordinary architectural space was the art. Carefully chosen and – gasp! – commissioned pieces by Charles Tyrrell and Mike Gale add an edge to the lobby and dining rooms. Elsewhere, lesser-known artists liven up darkest corners. There is no compromise in the beautifully furnished bedrooms, each of which contains a piece of contemporary, original art. The owners, architects and designers that worked on the Ice House are clearly committed to visual excellence and not afraid to put their money where their mouth is. Or perhaps they are canny enough to realise that compromising on art is not only crass, but unnecessary.

Because the truth is 'proper' art is everywhere in Ireland and it's available to everybody. We thought our art habit would ease when we decamped from Dublin to Mayo, but we were wrong. In fact, we have a found a great selection of national and international art available right on our doorstep.

We still keep the Dublin doors open. Paul Kane has such an eclectic mix of artists that are too in tune with our personal tastes to ignore. Paul knows what we like, his prices are good, he knows his stuff and we trust him.

The RHA annual exhibition is another Dublin must. Thousands of artists apply every year and an exacting panel chooses the winning work. There are hundreds of works for sale, with prices ranging from around €300 and to about €25,000 with the average around €2,000 to €3,000. Inclusion more or less copperfastens an artist's reputation – so it would be daft not to have a look.

However, regional art centres are the art world's best-kept secret. Most artists are very limited in the number of shows they can stage in Dublin. Those lucky enough to have a Dublin gallery will only expect to show every two to three years. Put bluntly, there are more good artists than there are galleries to support them. There are a few reputable regional art galleries in towns- the Claremorris gallery being one near us- but with many small-town galleries being more akin to framing shops selling touristy landscapes, local art centres such as the Linenhall in Castlebar and our own Ballina Arts Centre are becoming popular as gallery spaces for serious artists.

Seán Walsh, director of the Ballina Arts Centre, operates his twelve or so shows a year on the same principle as the RHA annual show. Applications for exhibitions are adjudicated and chosen by a different panel of artists and art-professionals. Past artists have included George Bolster, David Creedon and Chris Doris, and in the past few years my husband and I have been regular buyers. Frankly, we've been astonished at both the quality at some of the work and the lack of competition to buy it.

Seán is diffident and diplomatic when talking about sales but concedes, "Our biggest selling show every year is our annual Perspectives exhibition where we show the work of local artists. It's an open entry featuring the work of everybody across the board."

What he is saying, without actually saying it out loud is – it's bloody hard to sell art. But, hopefully, this is starting to change. When conspicuous consumption has become so deeply unfashionable so quickly, people need to find a new way to express themselves. While the Louis Vuitton luggage is being put to the back of the wardrobe, buying art has revealed itself as a classy, understated way to show that you have good taste and a few quid. Or, as Patrick Murphy says, "It's a good time to buy art, and a more pleasant way of enjoying some spare cash than putting it into a bank."

Some Do's and Don'ts:
Etiquette for the enthusiastic beginner collector
DO: Develop a relationship with a good dealer that you trust. Find a reputable gallery that operates within your price range.
DON'T: Buy something you don't like just because you think it will be a good investment.
DO: Ask to see what's in the stock room. Most galleries have more-or-less exclusive representation of the artist and if you don't like anything in the show, there might be something more to your taste out back.
DON'T: Haggle at an opening.
DO: Get yourself on gallery lists. Many send out invitations by e-mail and all have websites so an hour on the Internet should do it.
DON'T: Approach artists outside their gallery representative (unless they are friends/relatives). Most of them don't like it. If an artist sells direct from their studio – they'll either have a website or find a way of letting people know.
DO: Act on impulse. If you love something straight off, and the price is right, get that red dot up with your name on it. This is one-off stuff and once it's gone, it's gone.

On What We Eat

It's Tuesday . . . it must be fish fingers and chips tonight, because Thursday is Shepherd's Pie night, and Friday? Well, we're a bit posh here so we go all out with Mum's homemade curry complete with a handful of sultanas to give it that exotic, authentic feel. For pudding, we'll be putting hairs on our chests with jelly and ice cream or an apple tart and custard. Roll on Sunday with a nice bit of incinerated beef and Vienetta for 'afters'.

Anyone else long for those days back, when cooking a family meal was an uncomplicated daily affair undertaken by one member of the family (Mum) who would put up a reliable, if slightly unadventurous menu until Dad snapped and ordered in a Chinese? Why did it all have to change? Why did what we eat have to become such a complicated business? Deciding what to have for dinner has become a daily stress. It should be organic, of course, and, the latest fad, in season. (Lamb chops? At this time of year? Have you gone mad!) Every magazine we open is assailing us with bossy TV chefs telling us what we should and shouldn't be eating and when we should or shouldn't be eating it.

Rhubarb, game, all kinds of unpleasant sounding offal-type things... Day and night we should all be out foraging for mushrooms and gathering up elderflowers and crab-apples and sloe berries. They say, "Take a kilogram of sloe berries..." as if they were advising you to put the kettle on. What are 'sloe berries', would anyone mind telling me? And while we are at it you might look up "seasonal produce", which one Sunday supplement chef (a hairy Englishman...not our own lovely Rachel) suggested we stock up on for the month of November: cardoons, borecole, kohlrabi, salsify, scorzonera, wood blewits, pleurottes and, wait for it, hedgehog fungus. Delicious. He also suggested we rush out and purchase artichokes, grey squirrel, mallard, nettle, sloes, rosehips and quince. Quick . . . before Dunne's runs out of squirrel! Swede and turnips are also in season. And cod and goose . . . so it's not all bad news for November if you were planning on cooking and eating something.

Eating seems to have become yet another thing which we are all aspiring to do 'properly'. So that those of us who regularly plop fish fingers and oven chips in front of our child and who proudly serve our husbands for the third time this week with a dish which they foolishly professed their 'favourite' (lasagne in this house), as they smile weakly in reluctant thanks, feel as if we are failing.

It has become a complicated minefield of moral and social issues . . . leaking into other areas like social and sexual politics. Men do all the cooking on telly, why aren't they doing it at home? Am I a bad mother because my child will only eat "real" things that are white- rice, pasta and chips basically, and sometimes chicken, if it's first processed into the shape of a cartoon character he likes.

My sister is the editor of a posh food magazine (*olive* . . . it's great, buy it) and identifies herself as that new breed of person . . . a "foodie". A "foodie" is someone who "loves food". Not to be confused with a "fattie", who is someone who also loves food so much that they eat too much of it. She eats seasonally, and organically. She cannot tolerate incorrectly made coffee . . . and while she is, spiritually, a food snob, occasionally she is big enough to admit that my Lidl 100% Arabica coffee is "not bad", once served in the correct way, you understand. She is a challenging houseguest, but an educational one. (Boiled water left to stand for two minutes, warm pot, add coffee then water, and brew for four minutes before plunging).

Every time my other sister and I go visit her there are frantic emails to and from the UK as my two sisters and I plan our dinner in London. French? Portuguese? Gastro pub? Sardinian? We settled on a Japanese place near where she lives. The sushi is excellent but the service "patchy" so the other sister might get a bit fractious. She hates bad service. Whilst weighing up one sister's bad waitress stare against my own passion for sushi (which the county of Mayo has, sadly, yet to satisfy) it occurred to me that half of the world is starving while the other half is becoming pickier. Still, it's quite terrifying how quickly one can banish that thought when you've got a London restaurant to book.

As Marie Antoinette would have said were she alive today: "It's November... let them gather quince."

On Why Nuns Are Really Cool

I didn't even have time to write a column that week because I was so snowed under. I had deadlines looming all over and a builder was supposed to be coming that week to knock the wall through from my kitchen to dining room. But then… drama! … I got a phone call from a glossy interiors magazine to say they want to come and photograph my house. And that week was the only time they could do it to fit in with their deadlines. So I had to put the builders off, which I didn't want to do because they might go away forever and I might never get my kitchen dining the exact, proper way I want it. And, on top of that, I had to go up and down to Dublin in a day to have my new crown fitted, which, believe me, was the very last thing on my mind.

Did anyone care about my kitchen? Feel anything other than vague nausea at my "glossy magazines" name drop? How and when did I turn into this squawking nouveau hysteric? One of those boring women who divulge the minutiae of her sad, shallow life imagining she is entertaining?

A few weeks earlier I was in Kenya having dinner with a group of charity workers, including a couple of missionary nuns. They were both extraordinary women needless to say. Whatever your religious standing, whatever you think about the church as an institution, one cannot deny that missionary nuns rock. There's no two ways about it. It was the last night of an emotionally exhausting trip and, to be honest, I didn't have a lot of room in my head, or my heart, for any more bad news with regard to poverty, AIDS, genital mutilation, etc. I was feeling pretty wrung out. Therefore it was at my somewhat reluctant invitation that the nun I was talking to started telling me about her work.

She works in a country run by one of the more dangerous African dictators (which is why I won't even mention her name or his), where she helps give homecare to about 400 people with AIDS, more or less on her own. She cannot accept official funding, and has to operate under the radar. So a few people she knows in Britain and Ireland fundraise for her. She detailed with moving clarity exactly where so-and-so in Cork had a 30th anniversary party and put a hat around and so on.

The money gets put into a bank account in Dublin and once a year she comes over, takes out ten grand and smuggles it back into one the most corrupt and dangerous countries in the world where she hides it . . . under her bed, I presume. Every day this woman is risking her life and doing it with a kind of jolly humour that marks her out as one of those many missionaries who deserve a sainthood but will never get one because they are under the radar of whoever gives out sainthoods these days.

More than that, she was a nice woman, motherly and funny and warm. So when she said, "How are you?" it all came out. Every bit of nonsense I had been storing up for the past week. Not Kate, the caring individual with a social conscience, but Kate, the silly, spoiled housewife who's waiting to get her kitchen knocked and re-tile her worktops in case a glossy interiors magazine want to come and photograph her house. The nun nodded and smiled and appeared entertained. Afterwards I consoled myself by hoping I had provided her with some distraction from the hardship of her life. In actual fact I learned that what marks out a true saint is not just helping the unfortunate, but listening to the witterings of a pampered fortunate and making them feel like they matter.

On the Plight of Women

I love opening exhibits and have become rather adept at concise speeches about how important and lovely art is. There are nearly always a few Pringles, plus it's an excuse to get a blow dry and feel like a bit of a local celebrity. Although I know I am only on the B-list behind local county councillors, I nonetheless milk it, and have long perfected my 'standing next to the mayor' smile.

The exhibit at the local library was a one-off. A bronze sculpture by Elaine Griffin made from the casts of women's hands joined together to make a bowl. It's called 'Safe Hands' and was commissioned by Mayo Rape Crisis Centre and Mayo Women's Support Services. When the irrepressibly cheerful Ruth McNally, head honcho at the Mayo Rape Crisis Centre and general stander-upper of refugees spoke, her mood was uncharacteristically sombre.

The figures regarding rape are sobering. She noted that over the last three years 50% of the women who contacted their centre who had been raped were aged between 16 and 18 years old. They rarely report the crimes because they do not trust they will be believed, especially if they have any alcohol taken. "Are we really looking after our young women?" she asked, adding that it is easy for us to focus on early drinking and drug taking but when are we going to stop making it so easy to abuse a young girl and make the perpetrators who target them responsible for their actions?

We think of ourselves as being a civilised country, but the figures suggest that the number of actual rapes in Ireland is increasing while reported rapes and convictions are decreasing.

The year before I was in Kenya, a country where, while sexual crimes against women and children are endemic, women's groups are working hard to introduce new laws to protect them. If all of the measures they plan are followed through, the lives of thousands of women and children will be transformed. In the meantime we, one of the richest countries in Europe, have no plan in place because we are living in denial of the fact that the problem is getting worse, not better. We are giving the serial and opportunistic abuser carte blanche to abuse and rape on a regular and ongoing basis. If and when these rapists are brought to court, they are given lighter sentences than a shoplifter. We are becoming more civilised with regard to how many televisions we have and less civilised in the way we treat our women.

While everyone has sympathy for the raped, victims of domestic violence are still reviled. "Why doesn't she just leave? I wouldn't stay with a man who hit me. Imagine putting your kids through that?" To be caught in a cycle of domestic violence is surely the worst thing that can happen to a woman, not least because society holds the victim responsible for their own destiny. It is one thing to have a rapist jump out at you from behind a tree on your way home from Mass, but quite another to stay living in the same house as a violent man.

In this age of Girl Power, when we are emancipated enough to wear low-cut blouses to work and have IVF in our 50s so we can afford child-care, we perceive ourselves as being equal to men.

But they are still bigger and stronger than us, and they are still, like it or not, running the show. It is the bully that shapes the victim, not the other way around. At this time of year, it is important to remember that, for an increasing number of us, being a woman is, itself, a trial. The question is, what are the rest of us going to do about it?

MY PERFECT LIFE
(not!)

On the Five Circles of Clutter Hell

I am exhausted and depressed by my own inefficiency. Or rather, I am exhausted from the effort I put into being efficient and depressed by the complete lack of efficiency it results in.

There are five levels of clutter in this house. Level one is Everyday Clutter: the needless rubbish that gathers in my handbag, pockets, kitchen worktops, and coffee tables. Sunday paper supplements, unravelled dental floss, the dust of shells and small pine cones, paid bills, not-quite-ready-for-the-bin bits and bobs that stand in the way of my putting my hands on the things I really need, like cash, and unpaid bills and passports.

Then there is level two: Immediate Storage Drawers. There are at least two of these, full, in each room of our house where I put things that I use every day. A mish-mash of coins, packets of tissues, night lights - things that I would and should be using every day, if I thought to look in the drawers where these things are gradually stockpiling instead of forgetting where they are and buying them again. (Tins and condiments are the worst. I currently have six bottles of white balsamic vinegar, four large tins of pears and, annoyingly, I never stockpile things that I actually need, like ketchup or tinned tomatoes.)

I'll speed along. Level three: Out of the Way. This is the "useful" stuff that I never actually use and that has to be kept out of my husband's eye line or he will unceremoniously burn it while I am asleep. Foot-spas, camping equipment still in the box, bin liners full of fabric scraps - which I will someday sew into cushions - and air-beds, in case our entire extended family ever descends upon us at the same time and all the local B&Bs are booked.

In order of descending dreadfulness, level four is the penultimate layer of clutter hell: the St. Vincent de Paul Bags. These are things which I intend to give to the charity shop, but which still need to be sorted. Jigsaws and expensive kids' toys with bits that may or may not be missing, but which I will have to assemble to find out. Bags - and I mean a vast bin liner mountain of plastic bags here - full of grown-out-of and discarded clothes which I cannot yet pass on because they need to be folded/dry-cleaned and may possibly contain a jumper which my sister once admired and I must get around to asking her if she still wants.

And so we reach level five: The Attic. Until last week The Attic did not exist. So I pretended that I wanted it insulated and got a ladder and a bit of a floor put in while I was at it, so that now all of the unused rubbish in my life is literally hanging over my head like the sword of Damocles.

I long for clarity, a capsule wardrobe, a minimalist house, an organised schedule and a clear head with which to do my work, love my family and enjoy my life. And it's not like I don't throw out mountains of stuff every year; it's just that I acquire more with a speed that overwhelms me. It is with some shame that I have finally come to realise that, for all my good intentions at being environmentally friendly, I am little more than a huge hunk of landfill made flesh.

The reversal process is simple - stop buying pointless, worthless crap that I don't need and I will not only save time, money and the environment but might also fulfil a lifetime ambition of my own: one (1) allocated drawer for everyday bits so I can find a box of matches and a bloody pen when I need one!

KATE KERRIGAN

On Pretending to be Posher Than I Actually Am

When *Image Interiors* magazine came to photograph my house, I had one of those weeks where any semblance of denial about not caring what other people think of me was well and truly eradicated. If there is anything guaranteed to send someone with a mildly neurotic nature into a tailspin of ferocious house cleaning, it is the imminent arrival of an interiors magazine.

In all honesty I lost a week of my life gathering every vaguely aesthetically unpleasing object (which amounts to some 50% of my household goods) and hiding them in various cupboards, including the cavernous horror of our already piled-high attic. The toaster was, possibly, under an old duvet with a nasty avocado-coloured polyester cover in the linen cupboard. My husband was near nervous breakdown looking for important paperwork like tax discs and their like in Lidl bags. These bags contained everything from filthy make-up containers to kiddies' crayons to family portraits in bad frames and cheap shampoo bottles… in other words, anything that would have given me away as a normal person living in a normal house as opposed to a glamorous domestic goddess living a life of rarefied perfection.

"Why do you keep arranging to do all these things?" pleaded my frazzled mother as she watched her eldest child sob her way through cleaning out an anciently encrusted cutlery drawer just in case there was some test I had to pass beforehand. "They are not going to send somebody around to check your cupboards," said my sister. "Surely not," my mother said, but the two of them exchanged glances that said, supposing they do? What will she do then?

"I do it because it's fun!" I said, and they both looked at me like, "Yeah, right." They didn't say it out loud because they could see I had crossed over to the other side, into the place I went as a bridezilla and a first-time expectant mother: the Land That Sense Forgot.

The thing is, I love my house, and I have interesting bits and bobs and it's nice to celebrate them by having pretty photographs taken and sharing all my hard work. That should be enough.

Deep down I knew I didn't have to put my life on hold and my child into care so that I could rearrange curtains and commission co-ordinated throw cushions, and rearrange the books by my bed so that it looks like I read Balzac and Banville… but I did. Because while I pretend it doesn't matter, I care what other people think of me. I want people to think I have a nice house and a great life. It's not enough to just have a nice house and a great life… where's the fun in that? It's pure vanity, but believe me, one week of high-end neurotic cleaning is punishment in itself. In the end the *Image Interiors* team came and they were lovely people.

I needn't have worried, but worry I did. Passionately. Olympically.

When they were gone and I realised that I had expended far more valuable energy than I needed to have done, I collapsed in front of the telly. On the news I saw that a man had just been sentenced to four years for sexually assaulting a 10-year-old girl.

And my bedroom curtains aren't properly pleated? Isn't the world a funny place?

On Community

"Community" is the new lifestyle buzzword. We are all living too independently of one another, tucked privately and pod-like in small family units. I cottoned on to the whole "social capital" thing a few years ago and moved to a country village where, along with a great view at a great price, you get instant "community".

I was telling this, rather smugly, to a lecturer aunt of mine. She scoffed at my claims saying, "You live in a village and have a bunch of interesting friends. That doesn't make it a community."

"Yes it does, "I said, stupidly, seeing as she is an academic in the field of Community and Youth Work.

"No," she said, "that makes you part of a circle of friends. Not the same thing. A community is born out of a collective act or need."

"What if we babysit each others' kids and meet every Sunday for drinks?" I said, feeling my 'village community' fantasy slipping away.

"Lovely, "she said, "but it's friendship… not community."

Stuff it, I thought. She's wrong. My friends and I are a community . . . we are, we are!

When my son started school, I came to understand the distinction my aunt was making. It is the choice thing. You can choose your friends, but you can also unchoose them. You can't unchoose a community. A community is what it is and you can either be an active member or poke around at its edges, but you can't fundamentally alter it. Within the boundaries of the children my son went to school with, the parents of those children and the staff into whose care he went each day, I was trapped. I was lucky in that St Joseph's, Killala was a fabulous school and, admittedly, I am one of life's sandwich makers. I always laugh when people say they are "too busy" to involve themselves in community projects. In my experience truly busy people will always find the time to design a parish pamphlet, help tidy up the school art room, butter a platter of scones, run the youth club... because they are the people who are invigorated by doing. They are not doing it for the praise or the thanks... and they are partly doing it because it is what they do.

The week my son's school had its official reopening after a major refurbishment, Damian, the headmaster, called a meeting for parents to help prepare. Within days we had formed a supportive network of parents for the head and his team. I found the whole experience uplifting.

Marian, a lovely mum I'd never met before, came around with a picture she had found of the school choir in 1966 for the prayer book cover. Sam drove me into town in her big car and we wandered in open-mouthed awe around the cash and carry. I went into my neighbour Maria's kitchen for the first time for a brown-bread buttering marathon.

These social interactions are adventures for me- new people, new stories, learning about where I live and who lives around me.

When the day was over we sat around the school staffroom: a disparate group who had come together on that one day. We had no other reason to have gathered as a group and I thought this is it- this is a community. What we had in common was that we had answered the "somebody's gotta do it" call to community, which is like a dog whistle - some hear it and some don't. I felt pleased with myself, not just for the day's work, but for marking myself as someone who is a willing and proud member of my wider community... a sandwich maker.

On Ruling your Roost

I thank God every September when the kids go back to school. I adore my sons, and am one of those pathetic, doting, shmaltzy mothers who brandishes photographs of them at every opportunity. But even given my incorrigible, embarrassing attachment to my children as if they were the only ones in the whole wide world, by the end of a three month holiday with them I am ready (oh so very, very, very ready) to give them back into the care of the state for five hours a day.

My first official school summer holiday with my first son made it painfully clear to me how lacking I am as a parent. It seemed that manners and discipline are qualities that he has picked up in school and not from me. I needed him back there so that my threats to institutionalise him ("The police will come and put you in prison if you do that again!" and "It'll fall off if you keep doing that!" Fear and guilt are two under-used techniques in child-rearing these days) do not fall entirely on deaf ears. It had been a summer of indulgence; Nintendo DS games, long days in front of the telly, eating what you want when you want.

Like most parents of my generation I am great at issuing threats but have absolutely no follow through. Not a meal goes by when I did not remind him that soon, very soon, he would have to start eating proper food like a big boy and not simply bits of battered miscellaneous protein fashioned into funny shapes and doused in ketchup. Not a bedtime went by when I didn't remind him that soon, very soon, he would have to start brushing his teeth/let me wash his hair like a big boy because if he didn't… what? I won't feed him? I'd put him in a straight jacket and force a toothbrush down his throat? Drown him in bathwater and shampoo? Put him into a children's home? No. I'd say it again and again and again until he'd stop paying any attention to my hollow threats. Only he'd started doing it when he was just six.

I was, at least, not deluded enough to believe that my life was difficult with one child. It would be a cheek to believe, or certainly express, that a single child is hard work. But it nonetheless seems, if not fashionable, then at least acceptable to moan about one's children. I know people with two kids who complain constantly that they are "killed out" running them here and there, cooking for them, cleaning up after them… so much that you imagine they are rather troublesome houseguests rather than beloved offspring. However, I spare a particular kind of pity for those "career mothers" who decide to go for the "fertile, fecund, fabulously organised at 40" badge of baby number three. Six months later you see them looking hunted in Tesco negotiating a loaded double-baby seat trolley, blowing their bastard husband's salary on Tesco Finest ready meals because he's refusing to do the night-feeds third time around.

Most of our mothers coped with four-plus and no help. And we ate what was put in front of us and came out of it with decent manners. Having said that, they were the ones who fought for and got us the contraception pill.

On the Need to Do

Germaine Greer once made a convincing argument on telly about the fact women still "do" everything.

She reckoned men are driven largely towards the goal of doing nothing. This is why the (male) CEOs of big companies have huge, echoing offices. They sit at large empty desks and give orders for other people to carry out the actual work. Women on the other hand, she said, are compelled to "do" everything. So that when we said that we wanted it all - what we actually got 'all' of was the work.

Germaine Greer said that, not me. I wouldn't dream of denigrating the very important role men play in our society, the invaluable, essential contribution they make in the home and in the workplace. (Cough). However, I do agree that, generally speaking, women appear compelled to "do". While children have to be washed and houses hoovered, what my life is plagued with is the "doing" of things that I do not really need to be doing, the stuff which once I take the time to stop and examine it is just pointless activity. I have a job - writing stuff - and it keeps me busy. Then I have a husband, two sons, a house and various family commitments. That's enough - you would think - to keep a woman nicely occupied with perhaps a little time to lounge around in the evenings and weekends. If only I could leave it at that, instead of always trying to stuff more in, instead of always having to be "doing" something.

I'm not going to pretend I am one of these marvellous people who sits on tons of committees and runs around visiting hospices and organising fundraisers, who hasn't got time to brush her hair because one of her seven foster children has stuffed a towel down the toilet and flooded the house. The "doing" fuel that keeps me in perpetual motion is stupid tittle-tattle. Queuing in Lidl for cheap Yoga equipment, tidying cutlery drawers, sourcing un-needed and faddish cooking accessories.

The annoying thing is I have an endless list of valid things which would keep me busy for every moment of the rest of my life which I never get around to - tidying the garden, learning

Irish, shampooing the dog - and yet I volunteer myself for all this extra-curricular pottering nonsense as if I were a lady of leisure.

Of course, it is all propelled by guilt. One summer I decided to "do camping" for my five-year-old. I built him a fully functioning campsite in the field next door - working kitchen, play area, sleeping tent - the works. He sat resolutely in front of the television while I strung trees with homemade bunting like a mad person.

It's a form of neurosis. We've talked for years about getting a kitchen extension so we could expand our eating and cooking areas. On analysis I have realised all we would achieve is to create even more space for me to waste my time pointlessly moving things around in. I don't need a "walk-in larder" to house even more obscure tinned goods and, if I get one, it will need converting into a padded cell within six months. In fact, I am seriously considering throwing out every piece of kitchen equipment I have apart from the Breville and the kettle, and feeding my family on toasted sandwiches, tea and takeaways for the next 10 years. That way I can train myself to lie on the couch with a pizza box on my belly watching *Eastenders* for hours. CEO of my own sofa at last - just like Germaine's dream guy.

On How to Sauté your Brussels Sprouts at Christmas

"Christmas made easy. One hundred top tips to the perfect Christmas."

I tell you what would make my Christmas easier: if every newspaper and Sunday supplement stopped shoving Christmas down my throat from mid November.

"Ten Ways to Cook a Christmas Turkey"? One way will do actually, and here's a Christmas tip from me: if you are an adult person and you haven't figured out how to roast a Christmas turkey by now, go to somebody else's house for your dinner.

And here's another one - Christmas Wish Lists. "Our experts tell you what they will be wishing for this Christmas." Want to know what I wish for? I wish they would go away and leave me alone. All Christmas media is centred on trying to make me want more pointless junk to fill up my house and giving me more to do.

I discovered some years ago that Christmas dinner is, basically, a roast. I make one a week, and it really is no big deal. What makes it a big deal is Nigel Slater telling me how to sauté a sprout six weeks earlier than the event, the implication being that I had better start practicing and planning now.

Then there are the doom merchants. "Christmas can be a stressful time," they warn you. As for "How to Survive a Family Christmas", maybe I am one of a very lucky minority but I rather like my family. And, of those of them that I happily avoid all year around I do not feel suddenly compelled to cosy up to at Christmas, because that would be hypocritical bull. If you want to be a generous relative, throwing your doors open on Christmas day to some grouchy aunt and biding your time until you kick her out does not make you a saint. If you live in a 'civilised' country, then insane consumption is presented as nothing less than a public responsibility. Health service? No, what this country needs is for everyone to buy giant polyester sacks to fill with over-priced toys in unfathomable packaging and ghastly perfume coffrets.

In actual fact, I rather like Christmas. The hype is vile but the holiday itself is great. Holly, lights, and those lovely smelling-of-Christmas candles you can buy. In this house we even adore the turkey and ham aftermath. I adore how our house looks and smells and the routine of our gifts and our greetings, but a fortnight ago I drew down the attic stairs to get the decorations down and realised it was tragically early.

"Only three more weeks before we can buy the advent calendar and start counting down the 25 days to Santa coming, "I said brightly to my son.

"It's ages and ages away, "he said, quite correctly and crushed with disappointment. At seven, he was already learned that it is exhausting, expending energy and excitement on something before its time. That terrible build-up of pressure that has me frantically searching the shops for a pointless red velvet shrug to wear on Christmas Day because the pointless red chenille cardigan I wore last year went to St. Vincent de Paul in January.

Years ago I worked as beauty editor on a popular women's weekly magazine with really early deadlines and found myself producing "100 Ways to Sparkle this Christmas!" in mid-July. I compiled glitter and tinselly boob tubes and sexy Santa outfits in the midst of London summer heat.

The media claims it does not create public opinion; it merely reflects it. In which case I am the only person in the country not planning my Christmas table centrepiece before I've even taken the Halloween decorations down.

On Competition

Competitiveness is such an ugly thing. I once persuaded a very small (and probably terrified) child to admit that I looked younger than my youngest sister. I actually punched the air, delighting in my (much prettier, thinner and younger-looking) sister's deflation. My husband groans every time I invite people around to play cards. The whole experience is deeply stressful for him as he watches me transform from lovely hostess ("Vol-au-vent, anybody?") into a hawk-eyed cigar-chewing shark ("Yeah yeah, beer's in the fridge").

We all need a certain measure of it. Certainly I would not bother washing myself at all some days if I didn't have to face the stunning doctor's wife at the school gates, but too much is surely exhausting.

In the work arena I cannot imagine anything more debilitating or destructive than feeling that one is in competition with one's peers. For that reason, the only person I have ever competed against in my work is myself. I reserve my work dysfunction for co-dependent people-pleasing sucking up to agents and editors -much more useful.

I long since realised that it doesn't take nearly long enough for me to find somebody richer, prettier, more applauded and more talented than me and setting oneself up against the competition is not only foolish, but egotistical and self-destructive.

And yet competition as a mindset seems to be at the cornerstone of our lives.

Commerce needs competition to help it thrive, otherwise state-run telephone and energy companies would ride us sideways. But then when the earth freezes over, will we still be applauding ourselves for all those 99 cent Ryanair weekend breaks?

Competitive high-street prices are fuelled by sweatshop commerce. Third-world countries are being stripped of their culture; subsistence farming is being swallowed up overnight by huge multinationals so that they can provide us with bananas and coffee and five-packs of cotton knickers five cents cheaper than the next guy.

And then there is sport. I am a Mayo supporter, a sobering and by times character-building position to be in. I am still sore about losing to Meath in 1996.

I can still feel my blood boil when I think of Liam McHale being sent off and how we should have won that day and not had a replay and the injustice of it all. I can't watch Mayo play in front of other people. Everyone else goes to the pub but I have to stay at home in a darkened room, on my own, because the language out of me frightens children. When I meet nice, friendly people from Meath, I can feel myself not liking them because Meath (unfairly! unfairly!) beat my team at a football match over ten years ago. That's competitiveness.

It seems peculiar, then, that democracy is built on something so unattractive and potentially poisonous. Politicians campaign for our support by continuously undermining each other and tripping each other up. "Vote for me because the other fella made a balls of it!" Is it me, or does make-up and styling feature larger than ever on the election posters? One only hopes their principles aren't as slick and airbrushed as their election posters.

Political leaders need dignity to enlist the respect of the people they serve, yet the business of getting elected, all that squabbling and slagging each other off, exposes the worst of competitive behaviour. It may only be a game but it's hardly one that inspires nobility and respect.

On 'The Complaints Department'

"The complaints department is closed" is a phrase so over-used in our house that our son started to use it as a retort. "Come on and eat your lovely dinner?" I plead. "The 'Plaints department is closed!" he'd say. I suspected it wouldn't be long before he'd get the hang of "Eff off", like a normal five-year-old.

Perhaps it's because I am an ungracious receiver of complaints that I'm not a great complainer myself. I am a mutterer and so is my husband.

We sigh loudly in supermarket queues and splutter in quiet incredulity to ourselves over unavailable sundries, but actually forming our mouths around a public criticism… well that's just taking things a step too far. "Not worth it!" is the defence we use and yet it is, usually, worth complaining.

I know this because I have two English friends who are both magnificent complainers. One is mistress of the stiff letter to supermarkets in particular. "Imagine my disappointment when I drove an hour out of my way to your North London "Superstore" which purports to stock "everything" and discovered that there was no mascarpone cheese. Not so "super" now, eh?"

The other friend goes more for the brute force of a histrionic housewife. In Britain there are people trained to deal with people like her. Her proudest moment was in a well known chain where her failure to procure two jumbo packs of own-brand frozen cocktail sausages for an imminent barbeque sent her into a furious frenzy drawing a well-mannered young man fresh from a Customer Services management course from out back. He foolishly suggested that she might buy fresh cocktail sausages. "Do I look as if I am made of money?" she shouted at him, waving her brand new Nissan Jeep car keys gripped in fists made of expensively French manicured nails at him. "And," not content to leave it at that she added, "You have a very poor selection of shortbreads!" Not "no" shortbreads, you understand, but a "poor selection". That sort of detail separates the men from the boys in the world of customer complaints.

Her local supermarket has never seen her like.

One day their customer services man tried to placate her over a "sub-standard" bouquet with some free carnations. "Carnations!" she cried. "Are you trying to insult me?" He returned with two bunches of top-of-the-range lilies.

The area in which she lives is positively crawling with disillusioned English people who can't afford to live in Surrey and have moved to Mayo. They complain about the weather, the smell of silage and the fact that there is no Marks & Spencer… all of which is very, very annoying. But they also complain about the inflated price of things and the lack of mascarpone cheese and bad service. They ask for 'skinny lattes' in cafés that are still struggling to come to terms with the concept of the cappuccino.

And because they are so good at complaining, it means the nice local people don't have to. The other day I noticed my local café advertising chichi breakfast options. There is every possibility that a Mayo café owner decided there was a market for organic porridge with fresh-fruit compote all by himself, but I like to think there is some repeatedly complaining Brit marauding through Connaught towns demanding low-cal options for us all. Re-balancing the scales of history… one complaint at a time.

On Why Bunting Gets Me Going

It must be middle age, but the things that make me salivate with excitement these days are almost always to do with baking and/or bunting. In my 40s I feel much the same way about farmers' markets as I used to feel about getting dressed up and going to discos in my 20s or hanging out in posh hotels in my 30s.

So the prospect of contributing to the inaugural Killala Farmers' Market one Sunday nearly sent me into a mummified coma of pink gingham. Thankfully, I have a number of good friends involved who managed to persuade me not to give up my job and devote myself to making preserves full-time.

"Contribute to a community stall," Una said, staring at the confused co-ordinator as if to say, "Do not give this woman her own stall. I know her – she will take over." She's right, of course. I'm not a half-measures type. "No, we are not getting hens," my husband has had to assert to me at least once a week since the new River Cottage hit airtime. "Or a pig!" "But it will dig the field next door," I argued, "then we can eat it and grow vegetables in the muck!" Hugh Fearnley-Whittingstall has a lot to answer for in this house.

Despite only contributing to a community stall, I still went mad. Elderflower cordial, nettle pesto, brownies, lemon drizzle cake (I'm showing off now), mountains and mountains and mountains of stuff – and my four fellow 'stallies' the same. We co-ordinated by phone in the morning and agreed, we'd be taking most of it home again but it was a learning curve and better too much than too little. My neighbour Bernie had a dozen pots of her delicious cucumber pickle that improves with age, so she was happy to sell it over a few weeks.

In any case, it was lashing rain and the market would have to be held inside the community centre instead of outside, as we had planned, so that was sure to affect numbers. Chairwoman Maria was disappointed that the beautiful stands she had ordered wouldn't get an outing, but then it was decided to put them up inside instead and by the time we arrived, our cars laden down with produce, there was a little "café" set up with the animal rescue people doing tea and coffee and the hall was transformed.

They came in their droves. Niall Byrne had set his fresh fish stall at a side door and my sister and her husband bought it out – stunned at his fantastic prices, they rushed off with their chunky swordfish steaks fearful he had undercharged them. There was a beautifully laid-out organic vegetable stall – where my mother was able to buy garlic "actually grown in Ireland!" Sue's home-made Chinese ice cream and dumplings went down a treat, and every child in the place was baying for her delicious pancakes. Local artists at last got the chance to show off their work and our talented chef Derek sold about 50 litres of his legendary soups.

And as for us? We were cleaned out. Una's scrummy biscuits, Aideen's hand-tied fragrant herbs, every pot of Patricia's chutney, Bernie's relish and my pesto disappeared into the kitchens of our neighbours and friends.

At a time when so much of what we know as community is crumbling, the Sunday morning farmers' market is a place where everyone can come together and enjoy the fruits of each other's labours. It's a pretty wonderful feeling.

On Moonlighting as a Hairdresser

Thirty years out of the biz, I started doing a bit of hairdressing again, a little bit of pro-bono work… just for the sheer fun of it. Hairdressing was my first job, over half my life ago, and the only thing in which I can boast a formal qualification. I did not get on well in school, and hairdressing was the only career route left open to this 15-year-old rebel. I learned how to wash, perm, blow-dry, set… and being something of a colouring and chemical whizz, I ended up working in a glam salon in central London where I once did Cilla Black's roots and had the knee-trembling experience of neutralising Martin Shaw's perm.

Then I moved on. I became a journalist, magazine editor, author… yada, yada, yada. One of the things that has puzzled and annoyed me is that my move from hairdressing to media was perceived as "progression"- a move up, rather than across.

Having a trade young gave me a great start in life. I learned about money through working a till, PR and people skills by taking telephone bookings and talking to clients, good self-presentation (have you ever seen an unkempt hairdresser?), problem-solving (nothing seems difficult after talking your way out of a bad perm, even in the '80s) and the long hours gave me a strong work ethic. These things have stood me in good stead all my working life, and while I am sometimes conscious of not having had a third level education (to date, at least) I have never felt the lack of it in my career. I'm grateful and proud of my hairdressing heritage, and so, when my hairdresser Shona recently opened her own salon in the village, I offered her my services as an occasional help about the place.

Shona thought I was having her on but then one day, out of sheer desperation, she rang me (having sensibly taken the precaution of discreetly ringing around a few of my friends first to check if I could actually do hair and was not a deluded sicko, like the guys who walk around hospitals posing as doctors).

I had a great time. I did three very competent blow-dries and got a generous tip, which I promptly spent on sausage rolls and coffee from the garage… just like the old days. I went home with crinkly hands that smelled of shampoo, feeling very pleased with myself and creatively sated in a way I rarely feel after investing two years in writing a book.

Other peoples' reactions to my foray back into hairdressing have been revealing. There has been an assumption that it is somehow interesting and useful for me, as an author, to interact with "ordinary" people in this way.

Creative and/or media people who have never had "ordinary" jobs assume that they are somehow easier and use up less brainpower. As someone who has done both, I can tell you it takes as much concentration to negotiate an up-style as it does to write a column. And you have to do it standing up. And you can't change your mind and go back and re-do it in an hour's time.

They say books can change lives, and I've had people say that to me about my work on occasion. But ask anyone who's had a really bad haircut and you begin to realise that hairdressers have far more power over us than writers. I'm back in the salon in the next couple of weeks doing up-do's for a wedding. It's not research- it's real life. And I love it!

On 'Choosing a Nice Handbag' Awards

I once saw an advertisement for an American fizzy drink where we were encouraged to give people rounds of applause for doing ordinary but great things like buying knickers for your girlfriend or calling the guy to ask him out. Congratulations to everyone for all those little everyday things we do, which are brave and interesting and nice. It's lovely, but it does rather tap into this trend towards congratulating ourselves for doing nothing.

Award ceremonies are nice, feel-good experiences where people who are particularly brave, newsworthy or talented get to be acknowledged for their work. Of course the competitive elements of actually being an excellent hairdresser, or an exceptional actor, ballet dancer, writer etc is complicated somewhat by the competitive element of what you actually wear to the awards ceremony which has become almost as important as the awards themselves.

A good example is the VIP Best-Dressed Awards, where the women of Ireland are congratulated heartily, tearfully, for being able to put on evening gowns. The winner is given her full 15 minutes on talk shows all over the nation the next day, where she tells the nation she is still shaking with delight and how she feels honoured to be in the company of such glamorous women who know how to put on fake-tan, fake-nails and fake-hair. Everyone ooh's and aah's as she tells us her dress was aquamarine and had cost 1,800, but that it was her treat to herself and that today she is wearing a Madonna at H&M dress which cost 40 and that that was what style was all about.

I wouldn't want to take away her joy because winning anything is a lovely, lovely, experience and she almost always sounds like a very nice girl. But I do slightly despair that perky tits and fake nails and such fripperies are being held up as "achievements". Nobody is vainer and more of a self-obsessed fashion bore than me, but I do not consider dressing myself nicely and being able to apply lipstick or an even fake-tan as among my achievements in life. Actually, I consider it to be a terrible waste of time and money and the result of a weakness in my character called vanity.

Keeping oneself clean and tidy is having self-worth. Spending hours dolling oneself up to look like a Hollywood starlet every day is vanity. I do it, we all do it; it's fun. But it's like watching too much telly, or eating too many crisps, or smoking fags… it's a weakness. Giving women national media awards for spending all their money on clothes and knowing how to match their accessories is like giving men awards for sitting in front of the telly and drinking beer. "Here are the nominees for the men who dialled Domino's the most times in 2012!"

I'm just glad I have sons who can still look up to sports stars and academics and not a daughter who I have to somehow convince to study when her public role models are being rewarded for wearing expensive shoes. This constant, bleating pressure for "glamour" really is taking all the fun out of being emancipated for me. Perhaps the '70s chicks were right and a bit of bra-burning and hemp is the way to go.

Or perhaps it's just sour grapes because, actually, I go to an inordinate amount of time and trouble to dress myself and nobody has ever put me on their list!

On Being Unable to Resist a Hotel Buffet

I went back to Weight Watchers after the Sunday lunch buffet on my weekend away with the sisters pushed me over the edge. The last time I moved over to the dark side food-wise was after Kelly's hotel a number of years ago. Three nights and four days we were there. Our stay included breakfast, elevenses, lunch, afternoon tea – and then the thing that finished me off altogether- "kids' dinner buffet" at six. Two hours later, as a plethora of miniature cream cakes were sitting struggling with my big lunch for digestive space, I was firing delicious homemade chicken goujons in on top of them, and begging my already stuffed son to go up again because "it's free". By day three, I was waddling down to a gourmet dinner in my husband's tracksuit bottoms like a trailer trash American about to enter a bratwurst-eating contest.

Generally speaking, I can handle a breakfast buffet. There is an air of hearty optimism in eating early and everyone knows it's not humanly possible to stay in an Irish hotel without eating one's own bodyweight in fried meat before 10am. Otherwise what's the point? If watching your weight, you leave one rasher on the plate, then replace it with fruit, yogurt and cereal to compensate your system and keep everything 'moving'.

On your way past the breads table, you spot a pain au chocolat and grab one saying, "I'll have it instead of lunch." You eat it in the lift on the way up to your room to put on something with a looser waistband, but still, it's early. The day is ahead of you, and the good thing is that you are so stuffed you could not possibly eat another bite all day long, and you are going to go for a long, long walk and…

"Lunch? Are you mad?" I said to my sister when she said she had booked us into the Radisson Galway for lunch, after I had just finished inhaling a pile of creamy scrambled eggs, delicious, dark chocolaty wild mushrooms and half a sizzled pig. "I couldn't possibly eat lunch!" My mother and sister looked at each other. "You'll be hungry by two," my mother said. "It's a buffet," Claire said, then her face clouded with the realisation of what she had done. "Please don't torture me."

"With what?" I said, offended.

"With the running commentary," she said.

"I don't know what you're talking about," I said, "I'm just going to have a small plate of light salad, and some cold meats is all."

"Here we go," she said.

When lunchtime came, I took a small plate and headed towards the salad and cold meats section, announcing, "I'm just going to have a starter and that's it."

By the time the others sat down with their starters, I was up again "sampling" the smoked salmon and a couscous dish I had missed the first time around.

"Will I or won't I have a main course," I agonised for the next ten minutes. "I mean, it's paid for – and I could not have potatoes…" My sister tried not to involve herself in my torturous decision-making process but blinked, silently, in irritation.

I went up and had the full roast, and justified myself loudly and needlessly with every mouthful. Then, because I had already indulged, I sampled every pudding until I found one I was happy with – and made myself feel so thoroughly miserable I had to sign up to Weight Watchers again.

Too much choice makes me greedy and neurotic. The hotel buffet is a metaphor for modern life.

On Everybody Knowing Your Business

I was making the tea when I got a phone call from Mary, the owner of the local boutique in Killala.

"Sorry to disturb your tea," she said. I assumed she was calling to tell me the sleeves had been altered on the magnificent Christmas coat I bought there a few days before. I had been after a nice dressy red coat for years, and finally tripped upon The One while I was rifling through Mary's packed racks searching for an emergency evening dress for the "do" in London. Breda, who works with Mary picked out two black numbers and let me take them home to try on. This is why, I thought, standing in front of my own mirror, in my proper evening shoes, in the generous light of my own bedroom, I should always shop local. People know you. They'll stand you a pint of milk if you've left your purse at home and they'll trust you not to leave the country with their clothes stock.

"It's not the coat," Mary said, "it's just I've a sale on in bra's on and X was in and she spotted one here in your size and said I should put it aside for you."

This is what I love about living in a village, that a friend knows what bra size I am and told Mary up at the boutique. Also that she is able to intuit what time I have my tea.

This kind of intimate lifestyle is not for everyone. A friend of mine lived in a small village in Tipperary for a while and it drove her scatty. She finally put the house on the market when a neighbour called in to tell her, "You had a visitor earlier. Don't worry, I told her you'd gone shopping to Cork for the day."

"How did you know that?" my friend asked.

"Well – you were wearing your good coat and your new jeans so I knew you weren't going to the allotment, plus you had lunch out last Saturday and you'd never do that two weeks in a row." This was the same woman who, when gossiping over the fence with my friend about a mutual neighbour one day – stopped her as she was mid anecdote and said, "No, no, no, don't skim – I need the details! I want to know *exactly* what he said to you and what you said to *him*!"

My friend moved house, but I would have moved into her kitchen. I love knowing what's going on, and being part of the village story. Maybe it's because I grew up in an anonymous city that I find the very claustrophobic nature of village life so compelling. Of course, it's important to have nothing to hide. I'm not a closet boozer, or having an affair. I am, if anything, a bit too much of an open book, but I do find that is the best way, for me at least, to live in a village community. Of course I am judged – and if you get involved in community life as I have done, being on school committees and flogging my jam in the farmers market, you will put yourself up for comment. *"Look at her up there with her posh job and her big house charging €3 for a pot of jam."* I can only imagine what has been said about me, but, weirdly, I honestly don't mind. My grandmother used to say, "The only thing worse than people talking about you, is not talking about you at all." And I live by the proviso that I don't care what people say about me behind my back, as long as they are nice to my face.

Once, I put my head above the parapet and it got chopped off. I got up on stage after a school concert and said a few words to thank the teachers. I was nearly run out of town for speaking on behalf of the parents without consulting them first. I wouldn't have known or cared that I was the talk of every stalwart village mother, except that one of them broke rank and confronted me angrily at the school gates. It was unpleasant for everybody concerned but we all got over it and they were right anyway – nobody likes a big shot. Now I'm happy to operate the tea-urn from time to time and potter around the edges of village life picking up bits of news. Keeping yourself to yourself and minding your own business in a village is impossible and makes life a little dull. Also, I am naturally suspicious of people who are coy about sharing the ongoing story of their lives. I think – what's so fascinating about what you're doing that you can't share it with the rest of us?

Oh and the bra? A perfect fit and only €10.

On When The TV People Came to Town

"What's your address?" The Cactus television crew were calling to make arrangements to film me for the More 4 TV Book Club. They were booked into the Old Deanery Holiday Cottages in Killala with my friends Tony and Liz. The cottages are at the end of our road.

"I live in Kate Kerrigan's house," I said. "It's the last one before the pier – the one with the yellow door."

That is one of the differences between the English and the Irish. They number their houses and name their roads. Down here in the country we still assume anyone asking directions must half-know the place already. "Second left past the ball alley," and "three doors down from Gilvarry's" is the best we can do. Giving directions to tourists and visitors is a kind of vocational activity – it can take hours.

"I'll collect you from the airport," I said, "when are you arriving?"

"Oh that's very, very kind of you to offer," the young producer said, she sounded sort of non-plussed at the idea of it, "but we've booked a hire car. Is it far?"

The memory of my first year in Dublin, dropping a friend home to Mountjoy Square and ending up an hour later, in tears, in Stillorgan, flashed into my head. Mayo is a maze of confusingly directionless dual carriageways that turn suddenly into "old roads" and unmarked back-boreens that can carry you deeper and deeper into farmlands you think you'll never get out of.

"Not far," I said, willing myself not to force myself upon her like a deranged stalker, "about forty minutes away." Then, unable to help myself I squeaked, "but you might get lost?" I sounded like a child panicking the ice-cream shop might be shut.

"Oh," she said brightly, "we have sat nav." I stopped short of huffing, *good luck with that!* "See you Tuesday morning then. Around nine?" They were arriving in the village on Monday night. I'd see them well before then.

The English crew comprised a stunning young blonde called and a handsome cameraman, both of them were in their twenties. Everyone I work with seems to be younger than me these days but I have learned not to dismiss lack of years with lack of expertise or intelligence. Zoe and James were charming– full of flattering enthusiasm for my novel *Ellis Island* – and impeccably polite about the roast chicken and salad that I threw on the table to feed them on their first night. The weather was glorious when they arrived and they were looking forward to seeing some of our stunning scenery – they wanted to get some nice shots of "the author" (me!) walking down the beach looking wistfully out to sea, that type of thing.

In the morning the weather turned, and as we arrived at the beach there was a storm blowing. We pushed on and I walked up and down the shoreline of Ross beach, my hair plastered back from my face with rain, my drenched blouse (a ghastly silk mistake – I always panic when what I wear is important) stuck to my bosom, attempting an expression of thoughtfulness. As I picked the sand out of my teeth back in the car the young cameraman looked as if he was going to cry – his expensive equipment waterlogged and gritty with beach debris.

"We'll go to my mother's house," I said, "that's where I work anyway."

We headed to Mum's cottage in Ballina, and she and her visiting sister, my beloved Auntie Sheila, put on the kettle and got the good china out. We sat around and drank tea, and rifled through Mum's collection of old family photographs, then the camera followed me into the little cottage in my mother's garden where I generally write, wrapped in a blanket, the birds tapping at the tiny windows, pecking at the nuts my mother hangs on a hook outside.

It wasn't the magnificent scenic footage they dreamed off, but then, neither is my life.

My writing day comprises the chaos of motherhood, lots of cups of tea and interesting chats with my mam, and a bit of sitting down at the computer and banging out a few words in-between. I don't have the time to go to the beach and gaze wistfully out to sea. That's what I did in the days when I was dreaming of being a writer, when I imagined that that's what writers did. Now writing is something I do while domestic and family life buzzes on around me, shoving the baby's bottle into his mouth with one hand, finishing a sentence one fingered with the other. Distraction and stress and achievement, moments of panic and moments of peace – a lifetime in a day. Just like everybody else.

KATE KERRIGAN

On Organizing a Wedding

Helen is my writing partner, and when her eldest son, Jack, announced that he was getting married, the entire family waited anxiously for him to come back from Taiwan with his gorgeous bride, Rachel, so that we could celebrate their union, Irish-style, with a blessing and a big party in their barn.

Helen, the most gloriously laid back person in the world, was curiously and unnervingly tense. Mothers and weddings are rarely an easy mix, and Helen, unconventional though she is, proved to be no exception. She wanted the barn to glitter like a fairy-palace, she wanted a sit down meal for eighty, she wanted the swing set covered in fresh roses – everything had to be perfect. This was Jack and Rachel - no half measures would do.

The wedding planner in me lives very close to the surface. I had a *magnificent* wedding – but the best day of my life ten years ago has left me with a nagging, residual (and slightly insane) conviction that I know how to organize a wedding better than anyone else. I was itching to get stuck in, but Helen wasn't going to let me hijack her son's big day. I just couldn't see her pulling it off. I would have had the tables decorated a month early and sat with a feather fascinator in my lap – waiting.

Our relationship too valuable to upset, Helen and I kept a polite distance on the subject. Eventually I accepted my fate as mere guest and actually looked forward to my first wedding without succumbing to the aspirant bridesmaid weirdness that makes want to slap the drunk matron-of-honour and rush up to refresh the bride's lip-gloss between each course. I might, I thought to myself, actually enjoy myself like a normal person.

Then disaster struck. A day after they arrived in Mayo, Rachel had to go into Castlebar hospital. The whole family were up and down visiting and ministering - Helen's precious last week of wedding preparations were scuppered. We weren't even sure there would be a wedding.

What followed over the next few days was the most extraordinary experience of friendship and community. With Helen holding the reins - not for one moment letting go of her fairy-tale barn or her sit down, home cooked meal for eighty, or her rose covered gazebo – the family's friends and neighbours (and bossy writing partner) pitched in to make it happen.

It came together in a week. Dennis got out his whitewash brush and licked over the cottage and barn. Bernie and Sarah took over the food. Una, Sinead, Joan and Aideen K turned the barn into a fairytale palace (to Helen's infuriatingly detailed specifications!). Aideen W got her spade out and tackled the garden. I demoted myself from decider of favours to skivvy – I did Lidl runs, deep cleaned the bathroom and swept the stone floors of their beautiful traditional cottage and clapped the kids into tidying their rooms. I brought cups of tea and "hang sandwiches" out to the workers and revelled in the spirit of the traditional Mayo meitheal to make Jack and Rachel's day happen.

And boy did it happen!

Rachel came out of hospital the day before the wedding, all bright eyed and ready for action. She wore my wedding dress and already looked stunning in it before make-up artist Deirdre took her up a notch and made her glow like a goddess. Sabine provided the final touch with hand-made wild-flower bouquet.

Under the rose-covered swing the couple declared their love, while we all dabbed our tearful eyes and Niall took the official photos. We had trays of posh canapés prepared by Aideen K, and Una mixed the cocktails before the bride and groom were carried off in a horse drawn carriage, the children of the village chasing after them along Ross beach, ribbons trailing from the girls' bouquets, squealing and laughing like extras in a perfect wedding film scene.

It was a day not just for the couple, but for everyone that had worked on it. The satisfaction of belonging, of working for the common good was reward in itself.

When the ceremony was over, I abandoned my feather fascinator, replaced the heels with flip-flops and helped with the waitressing and washing up.

I missed Helen's husband Derek's speech where he emotively thanked all involved, but as I sat taking a well-earned breather behind the rose covered swing, watching the local kids play soccer in the heart shapes Dennis had mown into the lawn, I felt so happy to be a part of it all.

KATE KERRIGAN

On The IKEA Nightmare

I had to stop visiting the IKEA store near my mother's home in London because it caused a sort of hysterical rash brought about by too much choice. I would do that scary walk-around wanting everything tour, gathering dirt cheap, stylish, portable furnishings en route. Oh look – a plastic stool for 50p. Oh look – a cute table lamp for £1. A bag of 1,000 candles for 10p – I'll have those.

By the time I reached the till I was puce with excitement and a sort of heightened sense that my whole life was going to change irrevocably because of the two piled trolley of purchases I was struggling to push. I would have to throw out all of crockery to make room for the 90 plain white polish plates for 5p each, and I'd have to strip and polish the floors to show off all the new rugs – actually, come to think of it, I'd need to buy a new house with new windows for the mountain of muslin blinds.

After a full day in there, by the time I reached the checkout I would get an empty feeling of futility bought on by extreme consumer indulgence, and start to edit my purchases. "CD-rack? Don't need that. More cushions? Don't need them. Set of three vases? Not necessary."

On more than one occasion I would simply abandon the trolley, despairingly cram two Swedish hot-dogs in the yawning "having-shopped-and-failed" space in my stomach, before crawling out in the London rain, empty handed, to try and find a taxi along the characterless stretch of dual-carriageway that IKEA invariably inhabits.

And so, I avoided the Dublin IKEA like heroin, but as an addict, it was only a matter of time before it crept into my life again.

"We need cupboards for the back room," I said to Niall. The back room is the family Play Room – and as in all modern houses, that means Wii, computer, cable telly, DVD, stereos etc. Because it's where the children play we dump all our rubbish there, turning it into a non-safe play area – especially with the baby. Of course, he hared in there at every opportunity to shake the bottles on the precarious, flimsy bar and get the four teeth stuck in for a good chew on the trailing live electric cables.

"We need cupboards, cheap ones." We looked into every option and in the end, it was, of course, IKEA. "No," I said, "I can't do it." Then he downloaded the catalogue onto my laptop and I started to flick.

Oh my God. Here it was again. The opportunity, the promise that I could *transform* my life – all I needed was the right shelves. I could keep all that pointless miscellaneous crap that it crowding my life by simply hiding them away in MDF cabinets. The children's' rooms could be transmogrified into wonderlands with special display areas for their "art" and storage systems with brightly coloured plastic buckets which, somehow, look so much more appealing than the brightly coloured plastic buckets I have already filled their rooms with from the €2 shop. And it's all so cheap that we can decorate the play room, and afford a new flat screen telly with a built in DVD and get a man in to paint it first, and oooh! that rug would look great under the pool table and it's only €30 – and next thing I knew the day was gone and I had refurnished the whole house using the deadly "save and print shopping list" facility on the website.

Of course, what saved me is the fact that we live in Mayo, and would have to hire a van – and endure the horrendous palaver of driving across the country, then the two of us would surely have a nasty row brought on by my compulsive pottering, and the kids would be bored out of their minds and we'd have to placate them with Swedish hot dogs and all that – no, we'll leave it – too hard.

Except that somebody showed me an ad for One Man and His Van in *The Western People*. I contacted them for a quote and Fintan would go to IKEA with my list, buy everything and transport it down to us for €100. "One trolley load," he calculated my purchases at.

I didn't know whether to laugh or cry when I got the terrifyingly reasonable quote. He has made IKEA possible from the comfort of my own home. New novel? Who cares! Another column? What a bore. Hungry, tired children? For a week after it was, shut-up and go away the lot of you – Mummy is trawling through the website seeing how many combinations of shelves, sheets and sets of three vases she can fit on an IKEA trolley.

KATE KERRIGAN

On Making Sure I 'Mention The Book'

A researcher from the Marian Finucane show rang to ask if I would go on air and talk about an article I had written for *The Sunday Mail* about having a mid-life crisis. I had given up smoking two weeks (and three days and fifteen hours) before, and since then had gone into a state of frozen petrifaction over a new book.

I kept to my routine – Leo to school, Tommo to childminders, over to Mum's house in Ballina – put heater on in my writers hermitage in her back garden while I make myself coffee – then sit in front of the computer writing away until three. Except, instead of chuffing away on a half packet of Marlboro, churning out between one and two thousand words and emerging hours later with the guts of a new chapter and almost entirely unable to breathe, I am sitting gazing out of the window for five hours, barely able to squeeze out a single paragraph, wondering how many chocolate digestives I can reasonably eat without incurring a heart condition that is worse than the cancer I am praying I don't already have.

I don't want to smoke – starting again after six blissful years as a non-smoker was a physical, emotional and spiritual aberration for me. However, there is an evil little gremlin hammering away at my conscience trying to convince me of an evil equation: Input (ten to fifteen Marlboro Lights) = Output (a novel).

I knew it wasn't true. I had written big, long books with no fags before but the chemistry of sitting down and writing 100,000 consecutive words can be easily thrown off whack and frankly, my method of stubbornly sitting in front of the blank screen, sans fags, determined to slug the thing out wasn't really working as well as I'd hoped.

Normally a phone call to go on the TV or radio puts me into a state of panic and, when I am in the middle of a book and don't have the time to worry about what to wear and say in front of the nation, often results in a knee-jerk "no".

"Take a day off," my Mum said, "it'll do you good."

"Day off? Day off? I can't take a day off! Jesus – I have to have the first draft finished by Christmas!"

"Go," she said, "you've been working too hard. I'm worried about you."

Making my mother worry about me is less time consuming and somehow less self-indulgent than worrying about myself. Besides, I have my own kids to worry about – worrying about me is her job.

Anyway it wasn't genuine concern. She just wanted me to go on the Marian Finucane show. I could see her fingers twitching to ring Auntie Sheila: "She's on the Marian Finucane Show on Saturday." "No! This is it, Moira – she'll be *discovered*."

My Mum and her sister Sheila are my Greatest Fans and I am incredibly lucky to have these two inspiring, intelligent and lovable cheerleaders rooting for the Oscar or the Booker I am never going to get.

They were right, I decided, I should go. Besides, the panic of not writing for another day was worse than the panic of sitting in a studio with the fantastically intelligent and quick-witted figure of Marian Finucane.

Mum got straight on the phone.

"Is she talking about the book?"

"Hang on – SHEILA SAYS ARE YOU TALKING ABOUT THE BOOK?"

I called out from the kitchen where I was rooting for more biscuits and she relayed the info. "No Sheila – she's talking about Mid Life Crisis – or something. I know, I know – SHEILA SAYS MAKE SURE YOU MENTION THE BOOK!"

I didn't mention the book – and I did the stupid thing I do when I go to Dublin and put my heated rollers in on the train so that when I arrived in RTE my hair was so bouncy and crispy with spray that I was afraid it would interfere with the microphones and had to scrape it back into a bun. I was on the show with a gorgeous young guy called Patrick who runs a Creative Agency called Boys and Girls and has eight-month-old twins. He was talking about having "No Life" due to the times that are in it – but nonetheless living what life he has to the full. Marian was lovely to me as I talked about being a middle-aged wreck.

"Why do you put yourself down like that?" Mum said. Then she stayed up listening to the 3am playback and said, "I think she liked you."

"Don't be silly," I said, but secretly I was pleased. I felt grateful – for the mini-break – but also for having such a warm, everyday routine to take a break from.

KATE KERRIGAN

On Old Friends and New Years Eve

In 2010 an old friend came to stay for New Year. I hadn't seen Sue for maybe twenty years, and we had found each other again on the Internet. She's a very successful T.V make-up artist in London, full of fantastic stories about celebs and the state of their skin. Sue and I worked together and hung out together when I was in my twenties and living the high life of a glamorous young magazine editor in London. She reminds me of my beautiful years, makes real the myth of a youth that seems so long ago I can hardly believe it ever happened. A time when I was four stone lighter than I am now, full of energy and enthusiasm – absolutely gorgeous and yet tragically insecure and less confident than I am now as a crumbling middle-aged hausfrau.

Sue's daughter was heading back off to college in America straight after the Christmas break, so she thought she'd take the opportunity to pop on a cheap flight over to the middle of nowhere in rural Ireland. "It'll be nothing fancy," I told her, "just lots of lovely big dinners, and walks on the beach and hot toddies in the local pub." That's me being all low-key and self-effacing about our life here. I know it is absolute heaven to anyone living in the city. I know that because I used to live in the city and come here on holidays. On good days, I can still drum up the feeling that I'm on a country mini-break. When I can't, and am grieving for the fact that the stresses of real life follow wherever you go – even here – I can still pretend for the benefit of the visitors.

Weather permitting, she would arrive just in time for New Years Eve in our local The Village Inn. It's the only place I ever want to be to see the New Year in. Home in front of the telly is too lonely and depressing and a big fancy "do" is impersonal and too much of a hair commitment. The local means you can get all swanked up in the sure knowledge that all your friends and neighbours will see you, but at the same time be able to take your heels off and curl up in front of the fire and relax. Not everyone I love is there (my sisters and their families always go abroad for a month at Christmas which really annoys me – and my mother will be at home in her bed by ten) – but there's always enough of a gathering of mates to make me feel jolly, and my old friend Sue would be the icing on the cake.

This time the year before Niall and I were in the horrors. We were both still devastated by the sudden deaths of our respective brothers that year, and Niall's dad, Joe, was in Castlebar Hospital, critically ill. On New Year's Eve I had only one resolution: to survive the following year. Joe didn't make it, but Niall and I were still there, together, with our two boys.

"This year will be better," I said to Niall last New Year's Eve, "It'll be great."

"We still have a mountain to climb babe," he said – and he was right.

I was glad to see the back of 2010 – as will many people were, I expect. It had been a tough year for us as a family. We started with Joe's death, then we had illnesses and at a time when I was still emotionally vulnerable I found I was having to work harder than ever before to make ends meet, plus look after my family, which included a small child and a sick husband. That's the moan over – because everyone's personal plights were compounded in 2010 by the awful state the country found itself in.

In the past few months I had stopped smoking, got my sugar habit under control and even done two whole ten-minute sessions on the terrifying gym machine that had been hidden under a clothes mountain in my bedroom for the past three years. I had turned a corner and could at least see that, while we were within sniffing distance of the financial mire, we were not yet knee deep in it and, with a bit of clever plotting, might even be able to fill the fuel tank again before spring. I could finally see the top of the mountain we started climbing last year.

On midnight I raised a toast to, if not an entirely happy, then at least a grateful and resourceful 2011.

On The Polytunnel

Aspiring to country living begins with looking out your townhouse window at your fat neighbour getting out of the shower and *vowing* to replace your current view with one devoid of other people.

That done and a couple of years pottering about the village, boasting to city friends about the quality of local schools, tinkering about making jam for the farmers market one has finally had the last of the Cath Kidston sale fabric made into cushions and it is now time to get serious. The next step is self-sufficiency, the ultimate badge of the nouveau country wannabe – I speak, of course, of the polytunnel.

The year before we were out of our minds trying to score a bit of fresh coriander and coming home from the supermarket bemoaning the price and quality of slimy bagged salad leaves. This next year the Asian herb had already bolted and there was a veritable field of mixed greens for us to choose from. Was I feeling smug? Frankly, if I hadn't been me I would have hated myself. Hugh Fernley Whitttingstall is only trotting after us.

Reluctantly, I had to admit the polytunnel was not an entirely sole achievement. We share it with our neighbour, Steve, although that was my idea. I knew if we invested on our own it would quickly become one of our great family failures, going the way of the platinum gym membership- a life-changing lifestyle choice that came with great intentions and turned out to be a waste of money.

My husband used to be one of those men who would edge himself out the patio doors for the odd fag, shrugging himself cautiously against the bit of rain, doubtless still wondering just quite how in God's name he had come to live in Killala, County Mayo, when he had signed up for a life in Dublin's city centre with a media chick. Steve, on the other hand, is one of those energetic outdoorsy types, always mowing his lawn and calling to the door with handpicked mussels and going mackerel fishing, so I hoped he'd be something of a driving force.

As with most of my ideas I had sold it to my husband as a no-big deal thing. I have a terrible tendency to understate the amount of work involved in any outdoor activity I commission of him – my complete ignorance overtaken by unreasonable expectation. "It's only a *tree* babe – how hard can it be to trim a tree? Look, I've borrowed you a ladder and everything…." So, having booked the tunnel men to come and erect it for us, (and having cleverly absented myself from all real work by falling pregnant) all the men had to do was dig up a patch of land. Easy.

Or extremely difficult, as it turned out. It seems that the scrub grass growing on our narrow field was, in fact, an obnoxious weed whose roots had reached down into the earth's core. They hired every shape and type of man equipment from the man equipment emporium to no avail. Strimmers, rotavators, killer-grass cutting machines – until eventually they found somebody with a digger deep enough to wrench the triffid a few feet from its bedrock, and stop it growing for long enough to get the tunnel up.

Steve had, of course, already seeded his lettuces and planted them all in a neat row on his side. So, I had to quickly run to the garden centre and stock up on seedling greens, sprinkling a bit of compost over them so I could make them look convincingly home-grown. Other vegetable enthusiasts gave us various plants, which I threw down willy-nilly and with great enthusiasm, labelling nothing and hoping that every salad contained actual lettuce and not a roving, poisonous weed.

A year later it was a different story. My rain-reluctant, urbane husband had transformed into a Monty Don pin-up – all Hunter wellies and Barbour Jacket – out there every night watering and weeding and keeping evil slugs and weevils at bay. Every time I see him leave our back door, trowel in hand, full of stern intent to plant another lettuce, or attack a chard that's grown too big for its boots, I get a quivery feeling of marital contentment. I remember sitting in a married friend's kitchen in my early thirties and watching her husband mow the back lawn. I wanted what she had so badly – a kind man and a shed for him to potter about in – yet, at thirty-three, I thought I would never find it.

I assume like everyone that life is short, yet my life suggests it is long enough. I look back on where my life was before I met Niall and it looks so different now. Day by day, step by step, in small unnoticed increments, my dreams have come true. I've got a sexy outdoor-man in Hunters and a polytunnel full of fresh veg. Life doesn't get better than this.

KATE KERRIGAN

On Clearing Out The Shed of Shame

We had new doors built for the back gate and our dreaded Shed of Shame. Our friend Joe – a craftsman and carpenter – made them on sight, so his wife Rose came along. I needed her for the terrifying battle of emotional and physical endurance I was about to face.

"I need to clear that shed," I said, "but there's no way I can face it." The large concrete shed is where we throw everything that we cannot bear to deal with. It is the denial corner of our home.

The horror is layered. On the top layer are the things we just want kept out of sight because they remind us what we should be doing, but aren't. This includes never ridden bicycles, leaf-blowers, strimmers, spades, and plastic car covers. Underneath them are the failures – the enormous and expensive marquee that ended up in the top of a tree, broken furniture that will never get fixed, a child's tractor that simply ran out of batteries then was forgotten about – and beneath that again is the unspeakable carnage of mud, and insects and filth that time and complete lack of responsibility creates. Things that should have been thrown away and dealt with properly at the time that, over time, have transmogrified into a sludge so unspeakably awful that we would rather not just think about it. We are talking half-used bags of concrete and sand and compost spilling onto a damp floor that had stewed over years of neglect with old gardening gloves and never-planted bulbs and rotting boxes of recyclables that we moved from the house, to the patio, to the shed instead of just taking them to the dump when the box was full. The bottom layer of gruesome sludge has just been too terrifying to face, so for years we have just been opening the door and flinging stuff into it without even looking.

"I'll wait 'til the book is finished," I had said. "Then I'll tackle it."

And then, several books later, Joe took off the old door, and Rose and I stood on the threshold of my mountain of miscellaneous rubbish.

I went inside to make tea. I was thinking, sausage rolls from the garage and a pot of strong coffee while Rose counselled me over the shed. She'd put her arm around me, pat my back while we stood in joint horror at the enormity of the task ahead. Eventually we'd agree I should wait 'til the spring then find a couple of nice Polish men to come and put it all in a skip and take it away.

When I came out with the mugs of tea Rose had half the shed emptied and stuff sorted into recyclable, keep and landfill. "The dump closes at half-twelve," she shouted, "We have three hours – so start bagging up that pile of rubbish!" I put on my outdoor work clothes (a "distressed" jumper and jeans- christened as such because I am invariably distressed when I wear them) and a pair of work-gloves and got on with it.

Rose is a strong woman, with long, curly red hair and a "can-do" attitude – which is just as well as she can do and *does* almost everything she sets her mind to. She was the first female blacksmith to qualify in Ireland and, with her talented husband, virtually built their gorgeous house, and everything in it, from the ground up. At this time she was working full time in an accountancy firm and due to qualify in the next couple of years. Oh – and she has a son at Trinity studying medicine and the other son looked set to follow him. In their "spare time" the family ran an animal-rescue sanctuary in their home, and came to help friends clean out sheds!

Even if I had wanted to put her off I couldn't have, and so, in less than three hours we had filled the van to bursting point and Rose and I rushed down to the dump in our work gear, the damp stench of indiscriminate "stuff" for disposal emanating from the back of the van, not to mention our mulch-covered jumpers.

Not wanting to embarrass myself in front of Rose, I picked up pieces of wood heavier than myself and hurled them into sunken skips, wiped unidentifiable slippery gunge from my hands onto my jeans before picking up another double-bag of trash and throwing it in for landfill.

Back at the ranch we hosed down the filthy shed floor, and wiped what was left and put it back into place. Joe hung the new doors, and after my heroes left I flopped, soppy with exhaustion into a chair – and I thought to myself, "The shed is cleared."

My friends had made me a meitheal, and there was no way I could have done it without them. The experience reminded me that there is no problem too big to tackle – and we all need a good clear out from time to time. It's scary, it's hard work, but boy – it feels *so* good when it's done.

KATE KERRIGAN

On The Filthy Rotten Cigarettes

I was smoking again.

I won't give you my history; suffice to say in the past ten years I had been off the fags more than on them. I slipped during a depressive period after my baby was born, then I stopped for a few months, and then three weeks prior I had a storm-out row with Niall and went to my mother's house. While rooting in a drawer I found my old friend: the half smoked emergency fag butt. My mother keeps everything "just in case"- buttons, old safety pins, used BluTac, boxes of matches. *Why* she kept one of my half-smoked months old fag in her kitchen drawer, I can't imagine. Except, of course, it was me who had popped it away and she didn't even know it was there. I blamed her anyway, then in a fit of self-destructive pique grabbed it and smoked it down to its core. Weakness.

Actually, it's not. I'm not a smoker; I'm an addict. That means that I have a dubious relationship with all addictive substances. I gave up drinking at twenty after I realised that I did not have the inbuilt boundaries that even the wildest of my teenage buddies had – the radar for home, the alarm bell when a strange man asks you to meet him round the back of the disco. By the time I was twenty, having woken up from another terrifying lost weekend, a miraculous instinct made me take my finger off the self-destruct button, and not a drop of alcohol has passed my lips since then.

Sometimes people ask why I don't try drinking again. I was young, reckless, I have changed so much – how boringly temperate and anti-social to not share a glass of wine with the girls or take a sip of champagne at a wedding. I reply that the risk is not worth it. Why potentially trade everything I have for the occasional drink? Is alcohol really that important? Perhaps I could have the occasional social drink, but what would I gain from that against what I would lose if I couldn't? Besides, the reason I know I still have that compulsive inability to curb my habits is reaffirmed with my smoking.

In the three weeks since I had started again my priorities had altered back into the skewed world of the addict. Smoking is not a habit that had infected my life – life is now something that I do in between cigarettes. I'll feed the baby – after I've had a cigarette. I make phone calls because I am looking for an excuse to smoke, rather than smoking when I take a phone call.

The only saving grace is the wonderful smoking ban. It is now totally unacceptable to smoke – even in our own house – so that at least life has to stop when I smoke. As a young magazine editor I had a gag permanently on the go. The ash tray was full before my co-workers arrived in the office. I smoked and worked, smoked and cooked, smoked and socialised. At least now I have to go outside and reflect on what I am doing to myself.

I don't enjoy smoking. I don't like the way it tastes, smells or makes me feel. I dislike being a smoker. I don't think it's cool, or rebellious, or arty or amusing. It is vile. But my addictive instincts draw me to self-destruct, pull me into doing something to escape – something other than my life. Smoking makes me miserable, but still I do it. That is the mysterious thing about addiction that nobody really gets. *Why?*

My husband is disgusted with me, and nobody really gets that. He's a smoker, a heavy one. But it is not my health, or the ugly cut of me when I'm dragging on a fag that upsets him. It's the "other" thing. The fact that when he turns around to ask me something, or just to see that I am there, I am outside the back door smoking. I hide fag butts so he thinks I am smoking less than I am – rob fags out of his packet when my own supply runs low, say I have given up when I haven't and wait for him to catch me again. My addiction to smoking makes a liar out of me. When I am smoking, he is less important to me – and so are the boys. "I need to escape you," is what I am saying. "I'm somewhere else – smoking. You're not as important as this fag."

It's not the bad chest, or the coughing, or the diseases that will make me stop again. It's the mental and emotional power these nasty little sticks have over me. I had to stop again- and soon.

On Completing the Mini-Marathon

It's not very often that I feel like a hero - but on this day I did. Because on Bank Holiday Monday I walked a colossal ten kilometres on hard Dublin pavement, up and down the Stillorgan dual carriageway with some 40,000 other women. I was inordinately proud of myself.

It's peculiar where one's sense of achievement lies. A lot of people think that writing a book is an achievement, but I don't feel it as such. I am always thoroughly delighted when a novel comes out, but I feel it more as an achievement on my agent's part than I do mine.

Ditto my son. I am puzzled by people who view their children as "achievements"- it seems a horribly egotistical stance. Having children is a miraculous partnership of body and spirit as far as I can gather. I think of my child as an act of God rather than anything I've done. Hopefully I will rear him well enough to keep him out of prison but if he does end up a drug-dealing child molester I very much hope I shan't be blamed. Ditto if he becomes a brain surgeon. It will be his achievement and not mine.

As I reached the end of the mini-marathon (after an hour and a half of, for me, very brisk walking), I felt my eyes well up and my heart almost burst out of my chest with pride. The last time I felt this good was when I passed my driving test 15 years before. I guess it is something to do with doing things that you don't want to do.

I've always loved writing and being a mother was easy - but I was petrified of driving and only ever learned to do it because, as a young woman, I was entitled to a company car and my bosses pushed me into availing of it. Passing my test was a painful, frightening experience - so it meant all the more when it came.

A year and a half before this mini-marathon I was so unfit I nearly collapsed with exhaustion walking to the end of my road and back. Despair, age, and an expanding thigh-line brought me to Curves Gym in Ballina where Deirdre, the motivating

American who runs it, gradually whipped me into shape. Then last summer Sinead, my friend the PE teacher, started dragging me kicking and complaining on 5K hikes and I became addicted to the aqua-aerobics classes with Orla. The next thing I knew I had all these great women in my life to encourage me to get fit and healthy.

When Deirdre at Curves offered to do the mini-marathon to fundraise for a Kenyan girl's school I'm trying to support, I was daunted by the prospect. But in reality, the atmosphere, the sense of pride and community and social responsibility of walking with thousands of other women was immense - more that I could have imagined. I think I was probably the slowest woman on the Curves Ballina bus - we had a few runners and one or two exposed themselves as surprisingly competitive - but I believe I was the proudest.

This junk-food addicted heavy smoker became the sort of woman I never thought I would be - a reasonably fit and healthy one who could complete the mini-marathon without needing to be driven home in an ambulance. I was so swelled with pride that I had a real problem taking my medal off. For a few days after I had to keep my coat closed at Tesco.

On Having Two Names

I've got this prejudice against people giving their children 'unusual names.' It comes from the fact that my Irish catholic parents had their wild 1960's moment in the choosing of mine. Instead of wearing kaftans and smoking pot they 'broke out' briefly in 1964 and refused to call their eldest child Katherine or Anne after one of her grandmothers, instead calling me *Morag* Anne-Catherine after an arty friend of theirs. I was tortured at school. Tortured. And as groundhog hell every new person I have ever met in my life has said; "Morag – that's an unusual name?" To which I reply, "yes, it's Scottish" forcing us both into a pointless conversation about where I was born and why, which, since it is about me, leads the other person to believe that I am a dullard who believes that that the mundane details of my early life are simply *fascinating*.

A number of years ago I abruptly changed my novel writing style and my publishers decided to change my name.

At last - the chance to re-invent myself. I never liked 'Morag Prunty' as a name anyway. Ironically, it sounded made up. And sort of 'daft'. Echos of bully-boys laughing in the school bus "Towrag! Towrag!" I chose 'Kate Kerrigan'. It sounded warm, sophisticated and intelligent - much more like the real 'me'. The first couple of interviews were awkward. People would ask me a question putting 'Kate?' at the end of the sentence and I would look at them blankly – or giggle stupidly. When 'Kate' got nominated for Romantic Novel of the Year in London I was thrilled. At the same time I felt as if it were happening to a posh friend – and I, Morag, was going along as her uninvited guest. The short-list announcement breakfast was Kate's first 'big outing' and I made a special effort. No jeans and T-shirt as per – I picked out a long skirt and blouse, putting my hair up in a French pleat. "How do I look?" I asked my sister as I was leaving her house; "Do I look like a 'writer'?". "You should do," she said, "because you're dressed as Virginia Wolfe," snorting derisively at her own joke. Sisters are truly artifice sensors – the slightest whiff of pretension and they're on top of it.

At the event I wasn't allowed to be Morag – I was Kate. Recipes for a Perfect Marriage was Kate Kerrigan's first book (but in reality my fifth) and I felt vaguely awkward about the deception. But the end of the day, nobody cared whether I was Morag or Kate – it was all about marketing and perception. My proud editor took me around the room and introduced me to people I had met before and they didn't notice or care that I was a different person. I remembered what my mother had always told me when I was feeling fussy or self-conscious, "Nobody cares because they are too busy worrying about themselves," and realized, not for the first, nor I'm sure the last, that she is right. Very few people have the ability to thoroughly engage another human being if there is more than one or two of them around.

Now instead of saying "that's an unusual name" new people ask - "Is it Morag or Kate?"

Morag, I say, conscious that this is the same boring Scottish birth conversation in a different guise. Always was and always will be Morag, daft and all as it is. Perhaps there is something in a name after all.

On Bad Reviews

I had to wean myself off checking my book progress on Amazon this week. My latest novel Ellis Island has done well, generally garnered good reviews and had the accolade of being selected as a Channel 4 TV Bookclub Summer Read. But in the past couple of weeks a few nasty reviews have crept on to the web. I have always claimed to be immune to bad reviews – and for a writer, I know I am particularly thick skinned. I have never had a sense of entitlement around what I do, and as a result my writers ego is, I like to think, under control. I take criticism well, from both readers and editors, and almost every comment good and bad, is used to improve my work. I use every bit of feedback I can to progress my skills as a writer, but in any case, it is the creative endeavour that interests me more than the praise. I am pleased when people like my books, disappointed when they don't, but I am my own harshest judge anyway – so can't afford to take most of it to heart. Most importantly Ellis Island has sold well – which is the biggest statement of all. We writers like to be read, and we like people buying our books because – not wishing to denigrate or demystify the creative process – that is how most of us actually earn our living.

I love writing – it's an inbuilt passion, and I have always, and will always hold onto the feeling of privilege I get from being published in a world where so many brilliant writers are still working away in private obscurity. But frankly, there are easier ways to make a living. There are harder ways too, (I started life as a hairdresser, ten hours six days a week, varicose veins, tennis elbow etc.), but there is something particularly exhausting about devoting years to producing a book, day after day, slogging away on the longest most difficult school essay you have ever written. It requires a level of commitment that a writer aunt of mine once described as – "play a game of chess in your head", then having locked oneself away in this strangely private and often lonely pursuit – you have to prepare yourself to it being put out there in public, in the big wide world to sink or swim in a market already flooded with great books.

At first I found the bad reviews amusing. The expression "they are so bad – they're good" occurred to me. Then I found that when I sat down to write, the nasty comments started to creep into my head. I know I am not a terrible writer. In fact according to the professionals I work with – editors and agents, I rate myself rather less than I should. In fact, the only way to write is to not rate myself at all – just get on with it and do the best I can – like most working people. So this whole "one star" – "five star" business on Amazon is something that I tally with at my peril. Of course, I don't mind the five star reviewers - but this week I fantasised about giving the people who had written one stars about Ellis Island a taste of their own medicine. Standing behind them as they did their jobs and saying; *"God – you can do better than that surely. Call that a good job? You are woefully inefficient and insufferably dull. Oh, and by the way, that shirt doesn't go with those pants and you have a touch of halitosis."*

I was so enraged by one poisonous review that claimed I had written "a parody of romantic fiction" that I checked out their "other reviews" and was relieved to discover that they regularly bought a particular brand of sensible shoe (five stars) and was something of a gadget boffin. Social misfit – I said cruelly to myself – and undoubtedly falling into that category of person who secretly wishes they could write a novel but has neither the courage or talent to risk chancing it so they comfort themselves writing bad reviews for Amazon from their lonely bedsit.

Of course, that's probably not the case. They are probably a perfectly nice, well-adjusted, bookish person who is simply expressing their opinion, which they are perfectly entitled to do.

If I choose to spend my life writing books and am fortunate enough to get them published, then I must lay myself open to public criticism and comment. There is something distastefully egocentric in a writer complaining about bad reviews, but at the end of the day, we are only human. Even if the weird nature of our solitary job, and the level of obsessive self-confidence it takes to do it, sometimes suggests otherwise.

On "Being your own boss"

"Being your own boss" .It's what self-employed people say to other-people employed people to justify the stress and heartache of running your own business. "I may have a mortgage the size of a small South American country, and work eighteen hours a day but – hey – I'm my own boss!" Well I'm my own boss and I am thinking of firing myself. I had my hair cut yesterday. Nothing dramatic – just a fringe. What I would like to spend my five allocated writing hours doing today is contemplating and critiquing my 'new look' . Swivelling around in my office chair really quickly to catch myself in the mirror behind me. How does my fringe look when I am smiling? Frowning? Does it make the bits at the side look shorter, longer? These – *these* are the important questions on my mind today NOT – shall I remove this storyline altogether from Chapter Eight and what will it mean for my protagonist if I do – or, indeed, what can I interest the newspaper readers of Ireland with this week. My boss is shouting at me "No! You cannot waste a good days work looking at your fringe," but frankly, I can just put two fingers up to her – "Naff-off - what are you going to do about it you uptight old cow?" "Well," she says, "if you carry on like this our company will fall on its face, you'll never get the book finished, your agent will dump you, the readers of your newspaper column will write in and complain that you're wasting precious column inches talking about your fringe – you'll starve. Get on with your work!"

The problem with being your own boss is you can get away with nothing. When you have a boss who is not yourself, they are (usually) restricted by the boundaries of normal human behavior. They cannot perpetually tell you are rubbish and your children will starve if you don't work harder because – well then they would be put in prison. Also, occasionally they will leave the room and you will be able to recreationally apply lip gloss, or study your new fringe, or check out the New York shop Anthropologie website which is now mail-ordering from Europe (it's true!) without them being any the wiser. Bad bosses are frustrating and stressful, but in my experience however bad other people are to you, one is usually far harder on oneself. My boss (me) is perpetually issuing me with warnings of unemployment and imminent destitution. So that when I do whitter away precious work time dawdling and doodling I eventually become catatonic with guilt. Self-flagellating and worrying until I am so thoroughly bored with myself that I leave myself no choice but to actually sit down and write something. I'm not unusual. That's how most books get written – I am told. Some ponderous bores spend hours gazing at a sentence and pretend to be actually thinking when, in fact, they are just being ponderous bores. I am incapable of pondering. I fiddle, make corsages out of bits of paperclips and string – but it amounts to the same thing. Couple of years later I have a book that somebody paid me to deliver a year earlier. The truth is, we all need time to sit and gaze, and we've lost our natural lying-fallow time to the frantic "work ethic" of our age. I spend time looking at my fringe because my body and my brain need me to do that sometimes. I just can't give myself permission to do it. Think I'll go and ask my boss for a day off.

On Just Doing One Thing

It was dry and sunny yesterday so I ventured into the garden. The house was empty apart from the baby who was asleep, so I had an hour to myself. Within five minutes I was hysterical with stress. I picked up the phone and rang my Auntie Sheila in Fermoy. She is my garden mentor, although most of the time she has a therapy role.

"There are weeds and dead grass and rubbish everywhere. I have lost my special gardening stool/kneeler. My herbs are overgrown and dead. My rhubarb patch is grown over, my vegetable patch has gone to seed. I have six pairs of gardening gloves and they are all covered in mould – and yet I have no gardening tools apart from a children's set whose plastic handles have just snapped off. All my seeds are two years past their sell by date. There are two tents from last summer in pieces all over the back fence. There are drifts of dead leaves in every corner, probably with dead foxes under them. Can I put dead leaves in the compost? Can I put dead foxes in the compost? I don't know what's in my pots. What will I do? Where will I start? Help Me!"

Sheila, a keen gardener, attempts to calm me down. "You tackle the garden the same way to tackle everything – bit by bit – one hour at a time."

It mystifies Sheila that I can undertake the daily discipline of writing novels and yet I cannot seem to master the twice weekly task of pinching out my tomato plants.

When she asked after my tomato plans this year I exclaimed, "Blasted triffids! They took over the whole tunnel and *not one tomato*!"

"What about in pots? One bush tomato plant in a pot - then take it from there."

"No," I said, shaking my head, opening the lid of my composter to study my un-composted compost, "I can't do tomatoes any more. I put all that work into them…" I can hear her silent frustration coming down the line at me but I don't care, "…then they let me down. I have to let go of them Sheila. They're too painful. Tomatoes are out."

She takes a deep breath and brings me onto a more positive note. "How's your rhubarb?"

My rhubarb is my pride and joy. It never lets me down. I ignore and abuse it, but it keeps coming up, year after year, back for me. It is Rhubarb Who Loves Too Much.

"Flying," I looked across at my hardy plants – pushing up from their unmade bed of old leaves and bits of escaped miscellaneous plastic from the miscellaneous bits-of-plastic dump behind the composter.

"I love my rhubarb," I said wistfully, and for a moment, it seemed possible to garden.

"Do one thing now," she said kindly, "then come back again tomorrow."

I walked over to my dried out lavender bush and shuddered at the state of my herb garden. It seemed like only last week that I was down on my hands and knees clearing leaves off the ground beneath these plants, weeding through to the black soil, crumbling it with compost, mulching it, for goodness sake. And now look at it! Of, course, it wasn't a week ago, it was a year ago but surely, surely, it's not possible that I have to do all that work again? Of course I do because – newsflash!- stuff grows in the garden. It's not fair. Novels may take ages to write and longer again to edit, but once they are published you're finished with them. With the wretched garden you have to keep coming back and doing the same thing, over and over, year after year, again and again and again. It's not just a question of making it look nice. You have to go out there and keep it nice every day. For a completion junkie like me, somebody who likes to get the job done then wipe her hands and be done with it, gardening is a hellish occupation. And yet, for some reason, I am drawn to it.

I reached into the lavender and broke off a crisp flower head and rolled it between my fingers. It smelt exquisite and sweet. "Just do one thing," Sheila had said.

I went into my office and found an old, cloth evening bag, then went out to the bush, stripped it of its dried flower heads and made myself a huge, luxurious lavender pillow. Then I sat with the scented package on my lap and contemplated a summer full of fresh air, and falling petals – some of the rewards of my labour would be enjoyed this summer, and others not until the next year. It takes work to renew a garden, but, as with everything else in life, it's worth it.

AUTHOR'S NOTE

I had never considered compiling a book of my musings until a bright young intern from California called Lily Stoicheff came into my life. She had come from America to Ireland to be my assistant for a few months and the first job I gave her was the unimaginably awful task of putting my chaotic, crashing laptop into some sort of order. As a self-confessed "filing junkie" Lily started to categorize my columns and one day came to me and said; "You know – this stuff is *really* great. You should compile it into a book."

To which I replied; "You know I would... EXCEPT I AM TRYING TO WRITE A NOVEL HERE!"

Contrary to popular belief, writing novels is not always a process that involves lying on a chaise longue eating chocolates and looking out of the window musing and making stuff up. It involves deadlines and long, long stretches of words written one after the other that need to make sense - and be good - and tell a story. If, like me, you are working to publishers deadlines you are usually on a daily word-count that you have to hit whether the muse visits you or not. Writing novels is stressful, which is why every week I like to take a break from my imaginary world and write about the world I actually live in. Memoir is a necessary process for me as a novelist - it grounds me and helps keep me sane. However, ask me to compile my columns into something? Or put them into categories? Or even file them into folders onto my computer? Now – *that's* impossible.

However that is exactly what Lily did for me. As I toiled over my latest novel she filed, and compiled and edited and corrected a whole bunch of my writings – and turned them into this collection.

Lily was the final editor of the many who have encouraged, commissioned and corrected my work over the years. As a journalist and columnist I have been fortunate to have had my work published in a wide variety of newspapers and magazines over the years - from *Just Seventeen* (my first commission at age 19) to *Woman and Home* (my favorite magazine now as a menopausal mammy of two.)

Editing is a behind-the-scenes, often thankless task, so to all of the amazing editors who have commissioned me over the years: notably Finn on *The Sunday Tribune* (now sadly gone) Regina and Gillian on *The Irish Mail* and Ros and Helen on the *Sunday Mail* - thank you.

A special thank you to Lily – for infusing me with your youthful motivation and taking a whole bunch of my musings and turning them into an actual book.

Also thanks to Niall Kerrigan for cover photography and design and Martin Smith for proofreading and policing my punctuation.

Books by Kate Kerrigan

Recipes for a Perfect Marriage
(Pan Macmillan U.K. and in the U.S. Hyperion, as Morag Prunty)
The Miracle of Grace (Pan Macmillan U.K.)
Ellis Island (Pan Macmillan U.K. and Harper Collins U.S.)
City of Hope (Pan Macmillan U.K. and Harper Collins U.S.

www.katekerrigan.ie